DATE DUE

Faber, Adele + Mazlish, Elaine

How To Talk So Kids Can Learn

RA

BOOKS BY ADELE FABER AND ELAINE MAZLISH

Liberated Parents/Liberated Children

*How To Talk So Kids Will Listen &
Listen So Kids Will Talk*

*Siblings Without Rivalry: How to Help
Your Children Live Together So You
Can Live Too*

*Between Brothers and Sisters:
A Celebration of Life's Most Enduring
Relationship*

BOOKS FOR CHILDREN

Bobby and the Brockles

Bobby and the Brockles Go to School

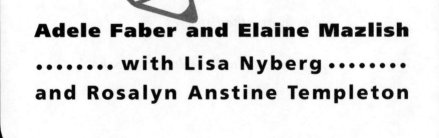

Adele Faber and Elaine Mazlish

.... with Lisa Nyberg ....

and Rosalyn Anstine Templeton

What every parent and
teacher needs to know

• •

HOW
TO TALK
SO KIDS
CAN
LEARN

AT HOME AND IN SCHOOL

Rawson Associates
New York

RA

RAWSON ASSOCIATES
SCRIBNER
Simon & Schuster Inc.
1230 Avenue of the Americas
New York, NY 10020

Copyright © 1995 by Adele Faber, Elaine Mazlish, Lisa
Nyberg, and Rosalyn Anstine Templeton

Designed by Hyun Joo Kim and Songhee Kim

Manufactured in the United States of America

10 9 8 7 6 5 4 3 2 1

Library of Congress Cataloging-in-Publication Data
How to talk so kids can learn—at home and in school /
Adele Faber . . . [et al].
    p.   cm.
Includes bibliographical references and index.
1. Teacher-student relationships—United States—Miscellanea.
2. Interaction analysis in education—Miscellanea. 3. Commu-
nication in education—United States—Miscellanea. I. Faber,
Adele. II. Title: What every parent and teacher needs to know
LB1033.H69   1995
371.1'023'0973—dc20   95-12131
CIP

ISBN 0-684-81333-5

How parents and teachers talk tells a child how they feel about him. Their statements affect his self-esteem and self-worth. To a large extent, their language determines his destiny.

—HAIM GINOTT

CONTENTS

Acknowledgments

The many people who believed in this book from the beginning helped it become a reality. Family and friends gave ongoing input and encouragement. Parents, teachers, and mental health professionals throughout the United States and Canada provided verbal and written accounts of how they had put communications skills into action at home and at work. Joanna Faber gave us many moving examples drawn from her ten years of teaching in an inner-city school. Bradley University and Brattain Elementary School lent their facilities and support. Kimberly Ann Coe, our illustrator, once again wrought her magic by taking our stiff stick figures and endowing them with life and warmth. Bob Markel, our literary agent, was always there for us with the right advice at the right time. Eleanor Rawson, our publisher, deftly and lovingly guided us to where she knew we had to go.

Finally, we wish to acknowledge Dr. Thomas Gordon for his original work in the field of adult-child relationships and, of course, our mentor, the late Dr. Haim Ginott. It was he who helped us understand why "every teacher should be, first, a teacher of humanity, and then a teacher of his subject."

How This Book Came to Be

The seeds for this book were sown when we were young mothers attending a parent group led by the late child psychologist Dr. Haim Ginott. After each session we'd drive home together and marvel at the power of the new communication skills we were learning and lament the fact that we hadn't known them years before when we were working with children professionally—one of us in the New York City high schools, the other in neighborhood houses in Manhattan.

We couldn't have predicted then what would grow out of that early experience. Two decades later the books we had written for parents had passed the 2 million mark and had been translated into over a dozen languages; the lectures we had given in almost every state in the United States and almost every province in Canada drew large, enthusiastic audiences; over fifty thousand groups had used our audio and video group workshop programs in places as far flung as Nicaragua, Kenya, Malaysia, and New Zealand; and all during that twenty-year period, we kept hearing from teachers about the changes they had made in their classrooms as a result of either attending our lectures or taking our courses or reading one of our books. Inevitably they urged us to write a similar book for them. A teacher from Troy, Michigan, wrote:

> After over twenty years of experience in working with disruptive, at-risk students, I was frankly

amazed at the number of strategies I learned from the books you've written for parents. . . . Currently the district in which I serve as teacher consultant is in the process of designing a new school-wide discipline plan. I strongly believe that the philosophy in your book should serve as the cornerstone of that new plan. Have you considered writing a book specifically for teachers?

A school social worker in Florissant, Missouri, wrote:

Recently I gave your "How to Talk So Kids Will Listen" group workshop program to parents in my district. One of the parents, who was also a teacher, began to use her new skills in her classroom and noticed a marked reduction in behavior problems. This came to the attention of the principal, who had been concerned about the increasing use of corporal punishment and suspensions in her school. She was so impressed by the changes in this one classroom that she asked me to run a workshop for the entire staff.

The results were dramatic. There was a sharp decline in "requests" for paddling, a decrease in suspensions, a drop in absenteeism, and self-esteem seemed to rise throughout the school.

A New York City guidance counselor wrote:

I'm deeply concerned about the growing number of children who are bringing knives and guns to school. I can't help thinking that more security guards and metal detectors are not the answer. But better communication might be. Maybe if teachers knew the skills you write about, they'd be better equipped to help these kids with short fuses handle their anger in nonviolent ways. How about a book for teachers, principals, parent volunteers, teacher aides, the school bus drivers, secretaries, etc., etc., etc.?

We considered these suggestions seriously but finally agreed that we couldn't take on the responsibility of writing a book for teachers. After all, we weren't in the trenches now.

Then came the fateful phone call from Rosalyn Templeton and Lisa Nyberg. Lisa was teaching third and fourth grades at Brattain Elementary School in Springfield, Oregon. Rosalyn was teaching future teachers at Bradley University in Peoria, Illinois. Both conveyed their distress at the coercive and punitive practices commonly used in schools to make children behave and said that for a long time now, they had been searching for materials that would offer teachers alternative methods to help students become self-directed and self-disciplined. When they came across *How to Talk So Kids Will Listen and Listen So Kids Will Talk,* they felt it was just what they had been looking for and asked for our permission to write an adaptation for teachers.

As we talked further, it became clear that their experience was extensive. Both women had taught in urban, suburban, and rural schools in different parts of the country; both had earned their doctorates in education; and both were in demand as workshop leaders at teacher conferences. Suddenly the project that we had hesitated to take on for so long seemed feasible. If, in addition to our own classroom experiences and all the materials we had collected from teachers over the past twenty years, we could also draw upon the past and present experiences of these two educators, then there would be nothing to hold us back.

That summer Rosalyn and Lisa flew in to meet with us. We all felt comfortable with each other from the beginning. After exploring the shape this new book might take, we decided to tell a story from the point of view of a young teacher who was trying to learn better ways to get through to her students. Her experience would be a fusion of all of ours. The narrative would be augmented by elements found in our earlier works—cartoons, reminder pages, questions and answers, and illustrative stories.

But the more we talked, the clearer it became that if we were going to give a whole picture of what it takes to educate a child, then we had to look beyond the classroom and give equal attention to *the first and permanent teacher in a child's life—the parent. Whatever takes place in school between 9:00 A.M. and 3:00 P.M. is deeply affected by what goes on before and after.* No matter how well-meaning the parent or teacher, if they don't *both* have the tools to help them carry out their good intentions, the child will be the loser.

Parents and teachers need to join forces and form working partnerships. Both need to know the difference between the words that demoralize and those that give courage; between the words that trigger confrontation and those that invite cooperation; between the words that make it impossible for a child to think or concentrate and the words that free the natural desire to learn.

Then it occurred to us that we had an additional responsibility to today's generation of children. Never before have so many young people been exposed to so many images of casual cruelty. Never before have they witnessed so many vivid demonstrations of problems being solved by beatings or bullets or bombs. Never before

16

has there been such an urgent need to provide our children with a living model of how differences can be resolved with honest and respectful communication. That's the best protection we can give them against their own violent impulses. When the inevitable moments of frustration and rage occur, instead of reaching for a weapon, they can reach for the *words* they've heard from the important people in their lives.

With that conviction, the project was launched. Three years and many drafts later, when we finally had the finished manuscript in our hands, we all felt a deep sense of satisfaction. We had laid down a clear set of guidelines for *How to Talk So Kids Can Learn—At Home and in School.* We had given concrete examples of the attitude and language that lie at the very heart of the learning process. We had shown how to create an emotional environment that makes it safe for children to open themselves up to what is new and unfamiliar. We had demonstrated how children can be moved to take responsibility and exercise self-discipline. We had shared a multitude of methods that encourage children to believe in who they are and who they can become.

It is our earnest hope that the ideas in this book will help you to inspire and empower the young people in your life.

WHO IS "I"?

When we set out to write this book, we decided to create one character, Liz Lander, who would speak for all of us. She would be the young teacher we once were, and her struggle to relate to her students in more helpful ways would mirror our own. She would be our "I."

1

How to Deal with Feelings That Interfere with Learning

THE MEMORIES OF MY OWN TEACHERS—
BOTH THOSE I LOVED AND THOSE I HATED—MADE ME DECIDE TO
become one.

I had a long, mental list of all the mean things I would never say or do to my students and a clear vision of how infinitely patient and understanding I would be. All during my education courses in college, I held on to my conviction that I could teach kids in a way that would make them want to learn.

My first day as a "real" teacher came as a shock. As much as I had planned and prepared, I was totally unprepared for these thirty-two sixth graders. Thirty-two kids with loud voices, high energy, and powerful wants and needs. Halfway through the morning the first rumblings began: "Who stole my pencil?!" . . . "Get out of my face!" . . . "Shut up. I'm tryin' to listen to the teacher!"

I pretended not to hear and went on with the lesson, but the eruptions continued: "Why do I have to sit next to him?" . . . "I don't understand what we're supposed to do." . . . "He punched me!" . . . "She started it!"

My head began to pound. The noise level in the room continued to rise. Words of "patience and understanding" died on my lips. This class needed a teacher who was in charge and in control. I heard myself saying:

"Cut it out. Nobody stole your pencil."

"You have to sit next to him because I said so."

"I don't care who started it. I want it ended. Now!"

"What do you mean you don't understand? I just explained it."

"I can't believe this class. You're acting like first graders. Will you please sit still!"

One boy ignored me. He left his seat, walked over to the sharpener, and stood there grinding his pencil to a nub. In my firmest voice I ordered, "That's enough! Sit down right now!"

"You can't make me do nothin'," he said.

"We'll talk about this after school."

"I can't stay. I ride the bus."

"Then I'll need to call your parents to get this settled."

"You can't call my parents. We don't got no phone."

By three o'clock I was exhausted. The kids burst out of the classroom and spilled out onto the streets. More power to them. They were their parents' responsibility now. I'd done my time.

I slumped in my chair and stared at the empty desks. What went wrong? Why wouldn't they listen? What did I have to do to get through to these kids?

All during those first few months of teaching, the pattern was the same. I'd start each morning with high hopes and leave every afternoon feeling overwhelmed by the drudgery and tedium of having to drag my class through the required curriculum. But worse than anything, I was turning into the kind of teacher I never wanted to be—angry, bossy, and belittling. And my students were becoming increasingly sullen and defiant. As the term wore on, I found myself wondering how long I could last.

Jane Davis, the teacher next door, came to my rescue.

The day after I poured my heart out to her, she stopped by my room and handed me her worn copy of *How to Talk So Kids Will Listen and Listen So Kids Will Talk.* "I don't know if this will help," she said, "but the skills in this book saved my sanity with my own kids at home. And they sure make a difference in my classroom!"

I thanked her, put the book in my briefcase, and forgot about it. A week later I was lying in bed nursing a cold. Idly I reached for the book and opened it. The italicized words on the first page jumped out at me.

> *Direct connection between how kids feel and how they behave.*
> *When kids feel right, they'll behave right.*
> *How do we help them to feel right?*
> *By accepting their feelings!*

I lay back on my pillow and closed my eyes. Did I accept my students' feelings? In my head I replayed some of the exchanges I'd had with the kids that week:

Student:	I can't write.
Me:	That's not true.
Student:	But I can't think of anything to write about.
Me:	Yes, you can! Just quit complaining and start writing.
Student:	I hate history. Who cares what happened a hundred years ago?
Me:	You should care. It's important to know your country's history.
Student:	It's boring.
Me:	No, it isn't! If you paid attention, you'd find it interesting.

It was ironic. I was the one who was always preaching to the children about the right of each individual to his or her opinions and feelings. Yet in practice, whenever the kids expressed their feelings, I dismissed them. Argued with them. My underlying message was "You're wrong to feel what you feel. Listen to me instead."

I sat up in bed and tried to remember. Did my teachers ever do that to me? There was that one time in high school when I was stricken over my first failing grade and my math teacher tried to give me a pep talk: "There's nothing to be upset about, Liz. It's not that you lack ability in geometry. You just haven't applied yourself. You have to make up your mind that you're going to do it. The trouble with you is, *your attitude is bad.*"

He was probably right, and I knew he meant well, but his words left me feeling stupid and inadequate. At one point I stopped listening and watched his mustache moving up and down and waited for him to finish so I could get away from him. Is that what my students felt about me?

Over the next few weeks I tried to respond more sensitively to my students' feelings, to reflect them accurately:

"It's not easy to choose a topic you want to write about."

"I hear how you feel about history. You're wondering why anyone would even care about what happened so long ago."

It helped. I could see immediately that the kids experienced the difference. They nodded, looked me straight in the eye, and told me more. Then one day Alex announced, "I don't want to go to gym and no one can make me!" That was enough. I didn't hesitate for a minute. In icy tones I answered, "You *will* go to gym or you will go to the office!"

Why was it so hard to acknowledge kids' feelings? At lunch I asked that same question aloud and told my

24

friend Jane and the others at my table what I'd been reading and thinking about.

Maria Estes, a parent volunteer, sprang to the defense of teachers. "There are so many children to teach," she said, "and so much to teach them. How can you expect yourself to worry about every little word?"

Jane looked thoughtful. "Maybe," she said, "if the adults in our lives had worried a little about *their* words, we wouldn't have so much to unlearn today. Let's face it. We're products of our past. We speak to our students the way our parents and teachers spoke to us. I know, even with my own kids at home, it took me a long time to stop repeating the old script. It was a big step for me to go from *'That doesn't hurt. It's only a little scratch'* to *'A scratch can hurt!'* "

Ken Watson, a science teacher, looked baffled. "Am I missing something?" he asked. "I don't see that it makes much difference."

I thought hard, hoping to come up with an example that would let him experience the difference for himself. Then I heard Jane say, "Ken, imagine that you're a teenager and that you'd just made the school team—basketball, football, whatever."

Ken smiled. "Soccer," he said.

"Okay," Jane said, nodding, "now imagine you went to your first practice session, filled with enthusiasm, and the coach called you aside and told you that you were cut from the team."

Ken groaned.

"A little later," Jane continued, "you see your homeroom teacher in the hallway and tell her what just happened. Now pretend that I'm that teacher. I'll respond to your experience in a number of different ways. Just for the heck of it, jot down what the kid inside you feels or thinks after each of my responses."

Ken grinned, took out his pen, and reached for a paper napkin to write on.

Here are the different approaches Jane tried with him:

Denial of Feelings
"You're getting yourself all worked up over nothing. The world isn't going to come to an end because you didn't make some team. Forget about it."

The Philosophical Response
"Life isn't always fair, but you have to learn to roll with the punches."

Advice
"You can't let these things get you down. Try out for another team."

Questions
"Why do you think you were dropped? Were the other players better than you? What are you going to do now?"

Defense of the Other Person
"Try to see it from the coach's point of view. He wants to produce a winning team. It must have been tough for him to decide who to keep and who let go."

Pity
"Oh, you poor thing. I'm so sorry for you. You tried so hard to make the team, but you just weren't good enough. Now all the other kids know. I'll bet you could just die of embarrassment."

Amateur Psychoanalysis
"Did you ever consider that the real reason you were cut from the team was that your heart wasn't in your playing? I think that on a subconscious level you didn't want to be on the team, so you messed up on purpose."

Ken threw up his hands. "Stop! Enough. I get the idea."

I asked Ken if I could see what he had written. He tossed me the napkin. I read it aloud:

"Don't tell me how to feel."

"Don't tell me what to do."

"You'll never understand."

"You know what you can do with your questions!"

"You're taking everybody's side but mine."

"I'm a loser."

"That's the last time I'll ever tell you anything."

"Oh, dear," Maria said. "A lot of those things that Jane just said to Ken sound like what I say to my son, Marco. So what could you do instead?"

"Acknowledge the child's distress," I answered quickly.

"How?" Maria asked.

The words wouldn't come to me. I looked to Jane for help. She turned to Ken and fixed her eyes upon him. "Ken," she said, "to find that you were cut from the team when you were so sure you were on it must have been a big shock and a big disappointment!"

Ken nodded. "It's true," he said. "It was a shock. And it was a disappointment. And frankly, it's a relief to have someone finally understand that simple fact."

We all had a lot to say to each other after that. Maria confided that no one had ever acknowledged her feelings when she was growing up. Ken asked, "How are we supposed to give our students what we never had ourselves?" Clearly, we needed more practice if we wanted to become comfortable with this new way of responding to the children. I volunteered to bring in some examples showing how we could acknowledge feelings in the school setting. Here, in cartoon form, is what I worked out and brought to my lunch buddies a few days later:

INSTEAD OF DENYING FEELINGS

When feelings are denied, a student can easily become discouraged.

PUT THE FEELINGS INTO WORDS

When negative feelings are identified and accepted, a student feels encouraged to continue to strive.

INSTEAD OF CRITICISM AND ADVICE

The teacher means well, but when a student is bombarded with criticism and advice, he finds it difficult to think about his problem or take responsibility for it.

ACKNOWLEDGE FEELINGS WITH A WORD OR SOUND ("OH" OR "MMM" OR "UH" OR "I SEE")

By responding to a student's distress with an attitude of concern and an occasional nod or "grunt" of understanding, we free him to focus on his problem and possibly solve it himself.

INSTEAD OF REASONS AND EXPLANATIONS

It's frustrating when a student refuses to respond to "reason."
What can we do instead? Is there a better way to help students
overcome their resistance to a task?

GIVE IN FANTASY WHAT YOU CAN'T GIVE IN REALITY

When we express a student's wishes in fantasy, we make it easier for her to deal with reality.

INSTEAD OF IGNORING FEELINGS

It's hard for children to change their behavior when their feelings are completely ignored.

ACCEPT FEELINGS EVEN AS YOU STOP UNACCEPTABLE BEHAVIOR

It's easier for children to change their behavior when their feelings have been accepted.

Ken looked at the illustrations and shook his head. "Theoretically, this all sounds wonderful, but to me it's just one more demand upon teachers. Where are we supposed to find the time to help students deal with their feelings?"

Jane's eyes twinkled. "You make time," she said. "Get to school earlier, leave later, rush through lunch, and forget about bathroom breaks."

"Yeah," Ken added, "and somewhere in between planning lessons, grading papers, developing bulletin boards, preparing for conferences—and incidentally, teaching—worry about what your students might be feeling or how to give them in fantasy what they can't have in reality."

As I listened to Ken, I thought, "Maybe it is too much to ask of teachers."

It was as if Jane had read my mind. "Seriously," she said, "I know it's a lot to ask of teachers, but I also know how important it is for children to feel understood. The plain fact is that when students are upset, they *can't* concentrate. And they certainly can't absorb new material. If we want to free their minds to think and learn, then we have to deal respectfully with their emotions."

"And not just at school, but at home," Maria added emphatically.

We all turned to look at her. "When I was about nine years old," she explained, "my family moved, and I had to go to a new school. My new teacher was very strict. Whenever I took an arithmetic test, she would hand it back to me with big black X's over every answer I got wrong. She made me bring my paper up to her desk again and again until I got it right. I was so nervous in her class, I couldn't think. Sometimes I even tried to copy the answers from other children. The night before a test, I always got a stomachache. I would say, 'Mama, I'm scared.' And she'd say, 'There's nothing to be scared of. Just do your best.' And my father would say, 'If you'd study, you wouldn't have to be scared.' Then I'd feel even worse."

Ken looked at her quizzically. "Suppose your mother or father had said, 'You sound very worried about that test, Maria.' Would that have made a difference?"

"Oh, yes!" Maria exclaimed. "Because then I could have told them about the black X's and the shame of having to do it again and again in front of the whole class."

Ken was still skeptical. "And that would be enough to make you feel less anxious and do better in math?"

Maria paused. "I think so," she said slowly, "because if my parents had listened to my worries and let me talk about them, then I think I would have had more courage to go to school the next day and the ambition to try harder."

A few days after this conversation took place, Maria returned, all smiles, and pulled out a small piece of folded paper from her purse. "I want you to hear some of the things my own children said to me this week. After I tell you, you must all guess what I *didn't* say to them. The first is from my daughter, Ana Ruth." Maria unfolded her paper and read: "Mama, my gym teacher made me run laps because I didn't get dressed fast enough and everyone was looking at me."

Ken answered immediately. "You didn't say, *'What did you expect your teacher to do? Applaud you? Give you a medal for being slow?'* "

Everyone at the table laughed. Maria said, "Now here's my son, Marco: 'Ma, don't get mad. I lost my new gloves.' "

"This one is mine," Jane said. " *'What?! That's the second pair of gloves you've lost this month. Do you think we're made of money? In the future, when you take your gloves off, put them in your pocket. And before you leave the bus, check the seat and the floor to make sure they haven't fallen out.'* "

"Hold it. What's wrong with that?" Ken asked. "You're teaching him responsibility."

"The timing is wrong," said Jane.

"Why's that?"

"Because when a person is drowning, it's not the time to give swimming lessons."

"Hmmm," said Ken. "I'll have to think about that one. . . . Okay, your turn, Liz," he announced, pointing to me. Maria looked down at her paper and said, "This is also from Ana Ruth: 'I don't know if I want to be in the orchestra anymore.'"

I jumped right in. " *'After all the money we've spent on your violin lessons, you're talking about quitting! Your father is going to be very upset when he hears this.'* "

Maria looked at us in amazement. "How did all of you know what I almost said?"

"Easy," said Jane. "That's what our parents said to us and what I still catch myself saying to my own kids."

"Maria," Ken said, "don't keep us in suspense. What *did* you say to your children?"

"Well," Maria answered proudly, "when Marco couldn't find his new gloves, I didn't lecture him. I said, *'It can be very upsetting to lose something. . . . Do you think you could have left your gloves on the bus?'* He stared at me as if he couldn't believe his ears and said tomorrow morning he'd ask the bus driver if he found them.

"And when Ana Ruth told me the gym teacher made her do laps in front of everybody, I said, *'That must have been embarrassing.'* She said, 'Yes, it was,' and then changed the subject, which is not unusual for her, because she never tells me anything that's going on.

"But the big surprise is what happened later. After her music lesson she said, 'I don't know if I want to be in the orchestra anymore.' Her words took the breath out of me, but I said, *'So, a part of you wants to stay in the orchestra and a part of you doesn't.'* She became very quiet. Then she started talking and it all came out. She told me she liked playing but that the rehearsals took up so much of her time, she never saw her friends anymore, and now they never even call her and maybe they aren't really her friends anymore. Then she began to cry and I held her."

"Oh, Maria," I said, deeply touched by her experience.

"It's funny, isn't it?" Jane said. "Ana Ruth couldn't tell you what was really troubling her until you accepted her mixed-up feelings."

"Yes," Maria agreed enthusiastically, "and once the real problem was out in the open, she got an idea for how to help herself. The next day she told me she decided to stay in the orchestra and maybe she could make some new friends there."

"That's wonderful!" I said.

"Yes," Maria said with a slight frown, "but I only told you the good things I did. I didn't tell you what happened when Marco told me he hated Mr. Peterson."

"Oooh . . . That's a tough one," I said. "Didn't you work in Mr. Peterson's class all last year?"

Maria looked pained. "A very fine teacher," she murmured. "Very dedicated."

"That's what I mean," I said. "You were in a bind. On the one hand, you wanted to support your son. On the other hand, you think highly of Mr. Peterson and didn't want to be critical of him."

"Not just Mr. Peterson," said Maria. "I'm probably old-fashioned, but I was brought up to believe that it's wrong to let a child talk against any teacher."

"But supporting your son," exclaimed Jane, "doesn't mean you have to disapprove of Mr. Peterson." She quickly sketched in her version of a parent's typical reaction when a child complains about his teacher. Then we all worked together on creating a helpful dialogue. Our challenge was to avoid agreeing with the child or putting down the teacher. Here's what we came up with:

INSTEAD OF CRITICISM, QUESTIONS, AND ADVICE

ACCEPT AND REFLECT FEELINGS AND WISHES

The bell rang. Ken picked up his lunch tray and said, "I'm still not sure about all this stuff. Maybe it's okay for parents, but it seems to me it ought to be enough for a teacher to be a decent person who likes kids, knows his subject, and knows how to teach it."

"Unfortunately," said Jane, walking out with him, "it isn't. If you want to be able to teach, then you need students who are emotionally ready to listen and learn."

I tagged behind, feeling there was more to say but not sure what. Driving home in the car that afternoon, I replayed the many conversations of the week and felt a new conviction growing within.

I wished I had thought to tell Ken:

As teachers our goal is greater than just passing on facts and information.

If we want our students to be caring human beings, then we need to respond to them in caring ways.

If we value our children's dignity, then we need to model the methods that affirm their dignity.

If we want to send out into the world young people who respect themselves and respect others, then we need to begin by respecting them. And we can't do that unless we show respect for what it is they feel.

That's what I wished I had said.

CHILDREN NEED TO HAVE THEIR FEELINGS ACKNOWLEDGED
At Home and in School

Child: Just because of a few careless mistakes, I only got a seventy!

Adult: Don't worry. You'll do better next time.

Instead of giving the above answer:

1. IDENTIFY THE CHILD'S FEELINGS.

"You sound very disappointed. It can be upsetting when you know the answer and lose points for careless mistakes."

2. ACKNOWLEDGE THE CHILD'S FEELINGS WITH A SOUND OR WORD.

"Oh" or "Mmm" or "Uh" or "I see."

3. GIVE THE CHILD IN FANTASY WHAT YOU CAN'T GIVE HIM IN REALITY.

"Wouldn't it be great if you had a magic pencil that would stop writing if you were about to make a mistake!"

4. ACCEPT THE CHILD'S FEELINGS EVEN AS YOU STOP UNACCEPTABLE BEHAVIOR.

"You're still so angry about that grade, you're kicking your desk! I can't allow that. But you can tell me more about what's upsetting you. Or you can draw it."

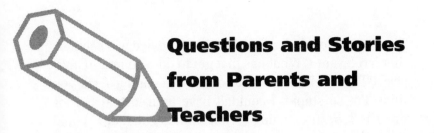

Questions and Stories from Parents and Teachers

Questions from Parents

1. Sometimes my seven-year-old son, Billy, falls apart when he does his homework. If he can't figure something out, he'll tear the paper out of his notebook, throw it on the floor, or break his pencils. What can I do about these outbursts?

Billy needs a parent who will help him identify his feelings and teach him how to deal with them. He needs to hear, "It can be very frustrating when you can't find the answer! It makes you want to rip and throw and break things. Billy, when you feel like that, say, 'Dad, I'm *frrrrrustrated!!* Can you help me?' Then maybe we can figure something out together."

2. For the past week, my thirteen-year-old daughter has been too upset to do homework or study for her midterms. It seems she had told her best friend in strictest confidence that she "liked" a certain boy and her friend lost no time in letting the boy know. After I commiserated with her over how betrayed she must have felt, I didn't know what to say next or how to advise her. What could I have told her to do?

One of the problems with offering advice—even solicited advice ("Mom, what should I do?")—is that when children are in emotional turmoil, they can't hear you.

45

They're in too much pain. Your hasty advice will seem either irrelevant ("What has that got to do with me?"), invasive ("Don't tell me what to do!"), demeaning ("Do you think I'm so stupid, I couldn't have figured that out for myself?"), or threatening ("That sounds good, but I could never do it").

Before your daughter can even begin to think about solutions, there are many concerns she might want to share with you: "Should I confront my friend? How? Can she ever be trusted again? Should I try to keep the relationship? Should I say anything to the boy? If so, what?" These are all thoughtful questions that give her an opportunity to understand more about human relationships. By moving in with instant advice, you short-circuit an important learning experience.

3. Is there never a time for advice?

After a child has been "heard out," you can tentatively ask, "How would you feel about . . . ?" "Do you think it would help if . . . ?" "Does it make sense to . . . ?" "What do you think would happen if . . . ?" By giving a child the option to accept, reject, or explore your suggestions, you make it possible for her to hear your thoughts and consider them.

4. Lately my son has been stomping around the house and griping about his social studies teacher: "He makes us read the newspaper every day and have debates every week and he's always giving tests. Nobody gives us as much work as Mr. M.!" I never know how to respond. It's getting to the point where I'm beginning to feel sorry for the kid.

Your son doesn't need your pity. He does need your understanding and appreciation for what he's up against.

Any of the following statements might be helpful:

"So Mr. M. really piles on the work."

"I can hear how much you resent all the pressure."

"I bet if you were the teacher, you'd declare a holiday every once in a while."

"Sounds as if Mr. M. is a tough and demanding teacher. It must be quite a challenge to live up to his high standards."

5. What can you do about a child who refuses to tell you what's bothering her?

As adults we have all had experiences that we haven't felt like talking about with anyone—for the moment or even forever. Some of us prefer to work through our hurt or pain or shame privately, by ourselves. Children are no different. They'll send clear signals when they want to be left alone to nurse their wounds. Even after hearing an empathic comment like "Something rotten must have happened today," they'll turn away or leave the room or tell you frankly, "I don't want to talk about it." All we can do is let them know that we're there for them if they change their minds.

Stories from Parents

THIS FIRST STORY WAS SENT IN BY A MOTHER WHO DESCRIBED how her husband helped their son deal with his "first-week-of-school" anxieties.

It was the second day of school and I was trying very hard to get my kids onto an earlier bedtime schedule. Everyone was cooperating—except Anthony, my nine-year-old. He kept whining and arguing with me and, no matter what I said, wouldn't get ready for bed. Finally I told my husband, "Joe, you'd better take over with 'your son' because I'm about to 'lose it!' " Here's what happened next:

Joe:	Hey, Tony, I want to talk to you. Mom says you're giving her a hard time. What's going on? Looks to me like something's eating you.
Anthony:	I've got a lot of worries!
Joe:	Well, I want to hear about them. All of them. Let's talk in your room.

They go into Anthony's bedroom together. Joe comes out about twenty minutes later looking pleased with himself.

Me:	What happened?
Joe:	Nothing. I put the kid to bed.
Me:	How'd you manage that?
Joe:	I wrote down his worries.
Me:	That's it?
Joe:	And I read them back to him.
Me:	Then what happened?

Joe: I told him I'd help him tackle his worries on the weekend and he put his list under the pillow, got into his pajamas, and went to bed.

The next morning, when I was changing Anthony's bed, his list fell on the floor. Here's what it said:

WHAT'S WORRYING ANTHONY

1. Messy closet and room. Not enough space to spread out.
2. Needs more clothes for school.
3. Great deal of work at school with lots of books to carry.
   (Too soon to start so much work!)
4. Needs more money for school snacks.
5. Something wrong with bike. Chain keeps slipping.
6. Lost quarter under washing machine.
   (Makes you feel even the little money you have is disappearing.)
7. Thinks maybe all money problems can be solved by father giving a hundred-dollar check.

I had to smile when I read it. You think only grown-ups have "real" worries. It's easy to forget that kids can have them, too. And just like us, they need someone to listen and take their worries seriously.

*   *   *

THIS STORY DESCRIBES HOW A MOTHER HELPED HER DAUGHTER get past her resistance to the college application process.

Almost everyone in the senior class had sent in their college applications, except my daughter, Karen. She's always had a tendency to leave things till the last minute, but this was going too far. I tried not to nag, to drop a casual reminder whenever I saw an opening, but got nowhere. Then her father sat down with her and tried to get her started. He was very patient. He went over some of the things he thought the college would want to know about her and even helped her to write an outline. Karen promised to get it all done by the weekend, but didn't.

As the days went by, I began to get hysterical and found myself yelling at her. I warned her that if she didn't send in her applications immediately, she'd never get into a decent college. Still no action.

Then in a moment of inspiration—that grew out of desperation—I said, "Boy, filling out a college application can be pretty threatening. Having to answer all those questions and write an essay that might decide which college you'll end up in is a job anyone would want to put off as long as possible."

She gave a loud "Yeah!!"

I said, "Wouldn't it be great if they got rid of college applications altogether and every college hired admissions officers who had ESP and would automatically know how lucky they would be to have you? You'd be flooded with acceptances!"

Karen broke into a big smile and went upstairs to bed. The next afternoon she actually started filling out her applications. By the end of the week, they were all in the mail!

* * *

THIS NEXT EXPERIENCE WAS SHARED BY A MOTHER WHO HAD TO cope with her child's serious, long-term illness.

When my son, TJ, was about eleven, he already had a pacemaker and special glasses to hold up his weak eyelids. Now he needed a hearing aid. As we drove home from TJ's audiology appointment, he announced, "You better not even get that stupid hearing aid. There's no way I'm wearing it to school. I'm just gonna throw it in the garbage. I'm gonna throw it in the toilet!"

As I drove, my heart sinking, I knew enough to keep my mouth shut until I could think of something to say that wouldn't make things worse. My son looked over at me and said, "Did you hear what I said?"

I replied (thank God), "I hear a boy who absolutely *hates* the idea of wearing a hearing aid—who feels that it is about the worst thing he can imagine!"

TJ sat quietly for a moment. Then he said, "Yeah . . . and if anybody at school makes fun of me, I'm never wearing it again!"

I paused and ventured, "Perhaps you'd like to have the barber leave your hair a little longer on the sides."

TJ said, "Yeah, let's tell him."

The pounding in my chest subsided, and I said a prayer of thanks for the skills I had learned.

Questions from Teachers

1. Is it my responsibility to deal with kids' feelings in the classroom? Isn't that the counselor's job? I barely have time to teach.

Sometimes what seems like the "long way" turns out to be the short way. It may be better to spend a few minutes dealing with a student's strong feelings than letting them mushroom into a problem that consumes valuable class time. In the process you will also have helped a child in need.

2. I get nowhere when I question my students about their feelings. They usually answer, "I don't know." Why is that?

Children become uncomfortable when adults interrogate them about their feelings: "What did you feel? . . . How do you feel now? . . . Angry? . . . Scared? . . . Why do you feel that way?" Questions like these cause children to shut down rather than open up. Especially unsettling to a child is the question that demands the answer to *why* he feels what he feels. The word "*why*" requires him to justify his feelings, to come up with a logical, acceptable reason for having them. Often he doesn't know the reason. He doesn't have the psychological sophistication to say, "When the kids at the bus stop teased me, it was a blow to my self-esteem."

When a child is unhappy, what he most appreciates is a parent or teacher who will venture a guess as to what might be going on inside him. "It hurts to be teased. No matter what the reason, it can hurt a lot." That tells the child that if he needs to talk more, the adult will be emotionally available to him.

3. You say children need to have their worst feelings accepted. Isn't there the danger that students will interpret our acceptance as permission to act out their worst feelings?

Not if we make a clear distinction between feelings and behavior. Yes, students have the right to feel their anger and to express it. *No, they don't have the right to behave in a way that harms another person, either physically or emotionally.* We can tell David, for example, "You were so mad at Michael that you tried to punch him. David, I can't allow any of my students to hurt each other. Tell Michael what you feel *with words, not fists.*"

4. I have a junior high student who comes from a dysfunctional family. It's hard for me to be understanding when he tells me, "I hate you," or "You're mean," or uses words that I wouldn't even repeat. I never know how to respond. Any suggestions?

Sometimes a troubled student will test his teacher by deliberately lashing out to make her angry or defensive. Part of the fun is to "pull the teacher's chain" and push her into a long angry harangue while the class smirks. Instead of reacting with hostility, you can quietly say, "I didn't like what I just heard. If you're angry, tell me in another way, and I'll be glad to listen."

5. One of my students recently told me about some troubles she was having at home. It seems her brother and her parents were always fighting. I said, "I can see how unhappy you are about that, but look at all the things you have to be grateful for." She burst into tears. What did I do wrong?

Beware the word *but*. It dismisses the emotion that was just expressed and signals: "Now I'm about to explain why your feelings are not important." Children need to hear an unqualified acceptance of their emotions of the moment. ("I can see how unhappy you are about what's happening at home. You wish everyone would get along better.") A response that conveys full understanding—without reservation—gives young people the courage to begin to deal with their problems.

Stories from Teachers

THIS FIRST STORY WAS FROM A STUDENT TEACHER WHO WAS assigned to a bilingual kindergarten class.

> Several weeks into the term a parent who had just moved into the neighborhood brought her little boy into the classroom, introduced him to the teacher, and quickly left. The teacher smiled pleasantly, showed him to his seat, handed him crayons and paper, and told him the class was drawing pictures of someone in their family. The little boy burst into tears. The teacher said, "No, no. *No llores.*" ("Don't cry.") I moved closer to comfort him, and the teacher waved me away. "Leave him alone," she said sternly, "or he'll be crying 'til June." Then she went back to her desk to finish her report.
>
> I tried ignoring him, but his crying was too pitiful to bear. I sat down next to him and gently stroked his back. He put his head on his desk and sobbed, "*Quiero mi mama. . . . Quiero mama!*" I whispered to him, "*Quieres tu mama?*" ("You want your mommy?") He stared at me through tear-filled eyes and said, "*Sí.*"

I said (in Spanish), "It's hard to leave your mother. And even though you know you'll see her soon, it's not easy to wait. Maybe we can make a picture of your mommy." Then I picked up a crayon, made a circle for a face, and drew a nose and a mouth. Then I handed him the crayon and said, "Here, you make the eyes."

He stopped crying, clutched the crayon, and made two painstaking dots. I said, "You gave her eyes. What color will you make the hair?" He picked up a black crayon and went on to make hair. When I left him, he was still working on his picture.

I felt wonderful. I guess I could have ignored him and he might have eventually settled down, but by acknowledging his unhappy feelings, I know I helped him to let go of them.

*   *   *

THIS NEXT SCENE WAS REPORTED BY A JUNIOR HIGH SCHOOL shop teacher. He told how he broke up a lunchroom fight by acknowledging the rage of each of the antagonists.

I heard yelling and saw two boys on the floor. I ran over and yanked off Manuel, who was sitting on Julio and pounding his chest. Here's what went on as I pulled them apart:

Me: Boy, you two are mad at each other!
Manuel: He kicked me between the legs!
Me: That hurts like crazy! No wonder you're so angry.
Julio: He punched me in the stomach.
Me: So that's why you kicked him!
Manuel: He took my potato chips.

Me:	Oh, so that's what made you mad. Well, I bet now that Julio knows you don't want anyone taking your chips, he won't do it again.
Manuel:	Better not.

They stood there glowering at each other.

Me:	Maybe you two need some time apart, before you can be friends again.

That was it. Later in the hall, I saw the boys walking together and laughing. When they saw me, Julio called out, "Look, we're friends again!"

* * *

THIS FINAL STORY CAME FROM A TEACHER WHO HAD TO COPE with students who were shaken by the outbreak of a war.

The day after the Gulf War broke out, many of the children seemed frightened and nervous. I thought the best thing I could do for them was to try to put recent events into a historical perspective, so I prepared a lesson reviewing other major wars the United States had fought, starting with the Revolutionary War. When I announced my intentions, the students were silent. One girl said, "Mrs. Ritter, could we not do what you planned today? Could we talk about how we feel about war?"

The class looked at me anxiously. I asked, "Is that what you'd like to do?" Heads nodded solemnly. I was touched that they trusted me enough to ask for an alternative to the planned lesson.

One of the boys started. "War is dumb," he said gloomily.

All eyes turned to me to see what my reaction would be. "I can hear how strongly you feel," I said. "Tell us more."

That did it. The next thirty minutes sped by as the students took turns expressing their worst fears and deepest anxieties. Then someone said, "Let's write. Okay?" "Good," I thought. "Maybe it would help if somehow they could channel their intense feelings into creative expression."

They opened their notebooks and wrote in somber silence. Toward the end of the period, I asked if anyone wanted to read his or her work aloud. Many of them did. Here are excerpts from the writing of three of the children.

> *Frightened and away from home*
> *they fight and lose their lives for*
> *something that could have been*
> *prevented.*
> >   *Silvia*

> *During war you hear many sounds*
> *sounds of guns or cries for help*
> *but the sound that is loudest of all*
> *is the sound of the breaking hearts*
> *of families of the men who die at war.*
> >   *Joseph*

> *Many innocent people will die*
> *and many more start to cry.*
> *When the children's mommies*
> *and daddies die,*

the children are sad,
the children are scared,
the children don't understand why.
                                    Jamie

By the end of the period, the heavy cloud that had hung over the room seemed to lift. The children had shared their common pain. We all felt more connected to each other. A little less alone.

2

Seven Skills That Invite Kids to Cooperate

DURING MY FIRST YEAR OF TEACHING, MY
IDEA OF HOW TO GET COOPERATION WAS SIMILAR TO THE NIKE
slogan: "Just *do* it!" After all, I had spent a lot of time carefully planning and segmenting the day into a series of
meaningful lessons. We had a lot of material to cover and
not much time in which to cover it. So if the class would
just sit there quietly and "cooperate," we would be able to
maximize our instructional time.

The word *cooperation* means *to work together toward a
common end or purpose;* however, I found that some of the
students acted as if their common purpose was to put an
end to my work! I'd be in the middle of reviewing a homework assignment when someone would ask for a pass to
the bathroom, a paper airplane would glide across the
room, and a student would fall out of his chair.

What was the matter with these kids? Didn't they know
how important it was to get an education? Hadn't they
made the connection between school and their own fu-
tures? Why couldn't they exercise a little self-control?

Then one day while on recess duty with another
teacher, I watched a group of students pushing, shoving,
and shrieking at each other over whose turn it was to
play with a ball. The teacher rolled her eyes with disgust

and said, "Look at them. They are so immature. What makes them behave so childishly?" I gave a noncommittal grunt, but to myself I thought, "Maybe it's because they *are* children, and maybe we adults need to be more understanding of how real children behave." When I met Jane in the teachers' lounge, I told her about my big insight at recess.

Jane shook her head. "What you're seeing is more than just childish behavior. Some of these kids are dealing with problems we never dreamed of when we were growing up. I have youngsters in my class who hardly ever see their parents. They're high-powered professionals consumed by their careers and desperately trying to 'do it all.' I have other kids whose parents *can't* be home, because they're holding down a day job and a night job just to survive. Ken has a child who has been in two foster homes and three different schools in one year. And you told me you have a boy who lives in a homeless shelter. Not only are these children coping with all the normal problems of growing up, but many of them haven't had a chance to be 'children.' "

Jane paused here and sighed. "The sad truth is that in today's world, kids are being subjected to unprecedented stress and neglect. If we're to have any hope of helping them master their academic skills, we have to help them unpack some of the emotional baggage they carry into our classrooms. That means our role as teacher has to change to include many elements of parenting."

I suspected Jane was right. Although some of my kids came to school ready and eager to learn, others seemed distracted and needful. Maybe that explained why they ignored or resisted my simplest request. Whatever was going on at home continued to drive their behavior in school. In a way it almost made sense. When Sam asked his mother if he could read his composition to her, she told him to leave her alone. (Her boyfriend had just walked out on her.) Melissa, whose widowed father was an alcoholic, was being raised by a teenage baby-sitter and a television set. She had no idea how to interact with adults. Eric's mother was chronically depressed. What would any of these children know about cooperation? They certainly weren't learning it from their families. Obviously I couldn't change what was happening in their homes. But maybe I could change what was happening in school.

As I thought about my teaching style, I had to admit that sometimes I sounded like a drill sergeant barking orders:

"Sharpen your pencil."

"Raise your hand."

"Put your name on your test."

"Stay in your seat."

"Get out your books."

"Keep your eyes on your own paper."

"Get in line."

"Lower your voice."

"Get rid of your gum."

"Be careful with the computer!"

Not only was I telling the children what to do, but I was also telling them what *not* to do:

"Don't run in the hall."

"Don't shove."

"Don't be rude."

"Don't hit!"

"Don't forget your homework."

"Don't write on your desk."

"Don't talk."

"Don't cheat!"

"Don't put your feet in the aisle."

"Don't tease the gerbil!"

Instead of teaching content, I was spending most of my time trying to control my out-of-control students. But if I didn't, how would they ever learn to behave in a civilized way? And yet it seemed that the more orders I gave, the more resistant they became. Precious class time was lost dealing with defiance and power struggles. On especially tough days I went home with my patience spent, my energy drained, and my strength sapped. I felt like the joke that says, "I have one nerve left . . . and you're on it!"

I went back to my copy of *How to Talk So Kids Will Listen* . . . and reread the chapter "Engaging Cooperation." All the examples took place in the home. What would happen if I substituted school examples? I jotted down my revisions of one of the exercises and brought them to school the next day to share with my colleagues at lunch. As they were drinking their coffee, I said, "Okay, gang. Let's play school—one more time. I'm the teacher; you're my students. As you listen to me, ask yourself, 'What did this teacher's words make me think or feel?' Then give me your uncensored reactions."

"No way," said Ken, putting out his hand for my paper. "I was the guinea pig last time. How about letting *me* be the teacher and you all react to me?" We agreed. What follows are the statements that Ken read and the reactions of the "students"—Maria, Jane, and me.

> *Teacher:* **(blaming and accusing)** You forgot your pencil again? What did you think you were going to write with? Now we have to stop class, waste everybody's time, and find you a pencil.

Students' reactions:	"I feel humiliated."
	"I never do anything right."
	"The teacher is mean."
Teacher:	**(calling names)** You have to be pretty stupid to turn in an assignment and not bother to write your name on it.
Students' reactions:	"I hate you!"
	"Everything I do is wrong."
	"I guess I am stupid."
Teacher:	**(threatening)** If I see one more spit wad, I'll pull you out of class so fast, your head will spin. And if this behavior continues, you're going to be suspended!
Students' reactions:	"I don't believe you."
	"I don't care!"
	"I'm scared."
Teacher:	**(giving orders)** Stop that talking. Put away your notebook. Get in a straight line. Now. Hurry up!
Students' reactions:	"I'm not your slave."
	"I'll do it, but slowly."
	"How do you get out of this prison?"
Teacher:	**(lecturing and moralizing)** It wasn't nice to break John's pen. How would you like it if someone broke *your* pen? If someone lets you borrow something, you need to take good care of it, just as you would want him to take good care of your things. Now don't you think you owe John an apology? I do.

Students' reactions: "I must be a bad person."
"Blah, blah, blah."
"I stopped listening."

Teacher: **(warning)** Watch those test tubes! They'll break and you'll get cut. . . . Careful with that Bunsen burner! Do you want to have an accident?

Students' reactions: "I'm afraid."
"I'd better not try to do anything."
"You're wrong. Nothing will happen."

Teacher: **(playing the martyr)** I go home every night with a headache because of you kids. Do you see these gray hairs? There is a gray hair for each one of you.

Students' reactions: "I'll buy you a bottle of hair dye."
"I wish I was outta here! I don't need this grief."
"It's my fault."

Teacher: **(comparing)** Why is your report late? I had your sister, Sally, last year and she always handed in her work on time.

Students' reactions: "I'll never be as good as Sally."
"I hate my sister!"
"I hate my teacher."

Teacher: **(being sarcastic)** No one remembers the year Columbus discovered America? Brilliant. This must be a magnet school for the dysfunctional. The only way to raise this class's IQ is if you all stand on chairs.

Students' reactions:	"I'm stupid. I can't remember anything." "This must be a magnet school. Look at the dysfunctional teacher we've attracted." "Go to hell!"
Teacher:	**(prophesying)** With your work habits, you'll never be able to hold a job. And if you can't get any better grades than this, no decent college is going to want you.
Students' reactions:	"It's no use." "I'm no good." "Why try? . . . I give up."

We stared at each other when the exercise was over. Jane voiced what was in our minds, "If *we* experience such anger and despair when we're just pretending to be students, what must *real* students feel?"

"Especially if they hear that kind of talk at home, too," Maria added. "My sister is always telling her children: 'If your grades don't improve, I'm taking away television.' 'You should study the way your brother does. Maybe you'd get A's, too.' 'You don't do your work because you're lazy.' She's always after her kids and their father is always lecturing them."

"My father's specialty was sarcasm," Jane said. "I suppose he thought he was being funny or clever. He'd say, 'Lost your library book? Well, that was a responsible thing to do.' When I was young that would confuse me. I'd think, 'How could losing something be responsible?' As I grew older, his sarcasm really hurt me and I found myself wanting to answer him back sarcastically. Sometimes I did. Unfortunately I got to be very good at it. When I first started teaching, words would just pop out of my mouth, especially when I was frustrated. I remember saying to one dawdling kid what my father had said to me a thousand times, 'Are you naturally slow—or is someone helping you?' The whole class cracked up."

"And that laughter," said Ken, "is music to a teacher's ears and what spurs us on to even greater heights of sarcasm."

"I know," Jane said solemnly. "But right underneath all the laughter is a kid who's being ripped up—publicly. I don't do it anymore."

"How did you stop yourself?" Maria asked.

Jane grimaced. "I take no pleasure in telling this. In my second year of teaching I had a particularly irritating girl in my class. In the middle of a lesson Theresa would think nothing of pulling out a mirror and fussing with her hair. One day I was questioning the kids about a reading assignment on ancient Egypt. Not a hand was raised. Then I spotted Theresa filing her nails. That did it! I said, 'Well, I'm not going to call on Theresa for an answer. She makes so many contributions to class discussions, we have to give someone else a chance.' A few kids snickered, but to my utter amazement, Theresa looked up from her nails and beamed at me. She thought I meant it! My 'compliment' had thrilled her.

"I was so ashamed that I said to myself, 'Never again! If I want to show my disapproval to a kid, I need to do it in a straightforward manner. If I want to be funny, I need to make sure that it isn't at a child's expense.' "

"Okay," said Ken, "so a lot of the things we normally say to kids either make them feel bad about themselves or bad about us. But the fact remains, it's still our job to see to it that they behave themselves."

"That's right," Maria added. "What should a teacher do instead—outside of trying to be nice and saying

'Please do this' or 'Please don't do that.' "

"Aha," I said, taking out my copy of *How to Talk So Kids Will Listen . . .* and waving it in the air. "The answer lies within." I opened to the chapter "Engaging Cooperation" and showed the cartoons to Ken and Maria.

Ken studied the drawings. "These are all home examples," he said.

"Yes," said Maria, "but kids are kids, no matter where they are, at home or at school. I don't think there's much difference."

"I think there's a big difference," said Ken, "between one or two parents dealing with one or two children and one teacher trying to control thirty kids at the same time."

"It's true. In that way the teacher's job is harder," Jane agreed. "In other ways the parent's job is harder. Theirs is a lifelong commitment. They can't dismiss their own kids at three o'clock. Or hope they'll get new ones in the fall. Nevertheless, whether you're in the living room or the classroom, the same skills can be very useful—and very effective."

For the rest of the lunch period, we all worked together at transposing the principles of engaging cooperation to the school setting. Here, in cartoon form, are the examples we came up with:

DESCRIBE THE PROBLEM

When teachers describe the problem, instead of accusing or giving commands, students are more willing to behave responsibly.

GIVE INFORMATION

When teachers give information, without insult, students are more likely to change their behavior.

OFFER A CHOICE

Threats and orders can cause students to feel helpless or defiant.
Choice opens doors to new possibilities.

SAY IT WITH A WORD OR GESTURE

Students dislike listening to lectures or long explanations. A single word or gesture encourages them to think about the problem and figure out what needs to be done.

DESCRIBE WHAT *YOU* FEEL (MAKE *NO* REFERENCE TO THE STUDENT'S CHARACTER)

When teachers describe their feelings without attack or ridicule, students can listen and respond responsibly.

PUT IT IN WRITING

Students often shut out adult talk, but if they see something in writing, they get the message. The sign below was placed on a dirty rabbit cage.

This note was posted on the assignment box by a teacher who was tired of giving constant verbal reminders.

A teacher sent this note to a student who was late handing in her term paper.

We were pleased with ourselves. The examples we had worked out together looked very doable—on paper. "Now, the real trick," I said, "is to put all of these wonderful ideas into action in the classroom."

"It may surprise you to learn," said Ken, "that on my better days I actually do some of this stuff naturally with the kids. I'm always telling them, 'Your feet . . .' 'The door . . .' 'Your reports . . .' Only I never knew before today that I was being 'skillful.' And there's something else I do that's not on the list."

"We left something out?" I asked.

"Yeah . . . fun. Play. A little humor. Anything to liven things up. I do it as much for myself as for the kids."

"A little joke is good," Maria commented. "Marco loves his biology class because his teacher always makes jokes. And it's true. On open school night the teacher told the parents that there's such a shortage of money that the first-period class may have to stitch up the frogs so that the second-period class can dissect them."

Ken laughed heartily. "That's what I mean," he said. "Humor puts everyone in a good mood and makes the kids want to cooperate."

I was curious. "What exactly is it that you do, Ken? Give me one example."

"Okay," he said, "fire drills. You know kids never take them seriously and how hard it is to get them out of the room. But if I do my 'Navy Command' routine, we're the first class out on the street."

"Your *what* routine?" we asked.

Ken rolled a piece of loose-leaf paper into the shape of a megaphone and held it to his mouth. "Now hear this!" he intoned. "This is a drill. This is a fire drill. Man your stations. Carry out your assignments. All hands on deck. On the double!"

"It's amazing how quick kids are to respond to anything that's a little playful," Jane said. "I remember when I taught first grade, it was always a battle to get everyone to line up to go anywhere. Then one afternoon I said, 'Children, let's make a train to go to recess. Juan, you come up front and be the engine; Monica, you go to the end and be the caboose; and all the rest of you will be freight cars in between. Now hook up to each other's shoulders and let's go!' In less than a minute they formed a perfect line and chugged on out the door—all smiles."

"But you'd only do that with little kids, right?" Maria said.

"That's what I used to think!" Jane exclaimed. "So when I was assigned to a fourth-grade class the next year, I thought they were too old for that sort of thing. Then one day I got a complaint from the teacher next door about how noisy my kids were on the way to the lunchroom. Instead of scolding, I told them—very seriously—to take their 'magic keys' out of their pockets, lock their mouths, and hand me their 'keys' before they walked out the door."

"And they did it?" Maria asked.

"Each one came up to me and put a 'key' into my hand. Then they all walked tight lipped and grinning until we reached the lunchroom. Then one at a time, I handed them back their 'keys' so they could unlock their mouths to talk and eat."

"Do your own children know how lucky they are to have you for a mother?" I said to Jane. "You must be so much fun to live with."

Jane smiled weakly. "My kids wouldn't agree with you," she said as she gathered her things to return to class. "By the time I get home from school, there's not much left of me. All I want is peace and quiet."

"And you'll have it," Ken said, walking out with Jane, "when your kids grow up and leave home."

That conversation took place on a Friday. On Monday Jane set her tray down on the lunch table and beamed at all of us.

"What's up?" Ken asked.

"I'm very proud of myself," Jane announced. "Remember what we talked about on Friday? Well, when I got home that afternoon, my kids were in the kitchen having their after-school snack, and there were books and sneakers and banana peels all over the table and crumbs all over the floor. Did I threaten? Did I call anyone a name? Did I lecture them? I did not." Jane paused here dramatically and pointed to Ken. "Instead, I used your idea," she said, "of speaking as if I were another character."

Ken looked bewildered. "Another character?"

"Actually," Jane said, "I tried a number of different characters. The kids loved it. And my husband got such a kick out of it, he came up with a few characters of his own."

"Give us a sample," said Ken.

"Here? Now? I'd be too embarrassed."

It didn't take too much urging on our parts. Soon Jane was entertaining us with her impersonations. Here, in cartoon form, are the characters Jane and her husband created for their own amusement and that of their children:

INSTEAD OF SCOLDING

TRY USING ANOTHER VOICE OR ACCENT

SOUTHERN BELLE

Ah do declare, ah'm 'bout to swoon from the disorder in this kitchen. Y'all come lend a hand now!

GANGSTER

Okay you guys, dis dump better be cleaned up before chow time or dere's gonna be BIG TROUBLE!

OPERA SINGER

The crumbs, the crumbs. I feel crummy from these crumbs.

ENGLISH LORD

I say old chaps, dinner will be served at six. Do tidy up so we can dine in comfort

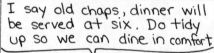

ROBOT

All --- toys --- books --- shoes --- banana peels --- need --- to --- vanish --- before --- dinner.

FRENCH MAID

Mon dieu! Sneaker on zee table where we eat? No, no, no, no, no. Zee sneakers zey belong in zee closet.

Maria couldn't stop smiling. "What you did was very funny," she said. "And I know if I pretended with my children that way, they would probably clean up, too. But I would feel foolish. That's not the kind of person I am. I'm more serious. Maybe too serious."

"I don't know about that," Jane said. "I think we all have a playful part of us locked away somewhere. We just need to locate it and let it out. Look what you did with Ana Ruth the other morning."

Maria looked puzzled.

"When you had that big fight before she left for school."

Maria blushed. "Oh, that was nothing."

"Trust me," Jane said. "It was something. Tell them all what happened. Please."

Maria hesitated a moment. "Well, Ana Ruth and I had this bad argument right before the bus was coming. I could see how much it upset her to leave before we made up. I knew she wanted to kiss me but also that she didn't want to. So I asked her if I could have a kiss. She said, 'No!' I asked her if I could have a kiss when she came home from school. She said, 'No!' So I asked her if I could have a kiss when she got married! She laughed and said, 'Oh, Mom,' and gave me a hug and a kiss and we both felt better."

At the end of the lunch period I found myself feeling strangely elated as I climbed the stairs to my classroom. I was touched by Maria's story (imagine being playful at such a tense moment!) and charmed by the crazy characters Jane and her husband had invented. It sounded like such fun to try something different, to do the unexpected. I thought about the rambunctious kids in my class who continually called out their answers without raising their hands. I had tried many of my new skills with them, but never humor. I had described the problem: *"I hear answers, but I don't see hands."* That worked with some of the children. I told them what I felt. *"It frustrates me when everyone calls out at once and I wind up hearing no one."* A few more responded appropriately. To the holdouts I offered a choice: *"You can raise your left hand or your right hand."* Some chose right; some chose left; one put up both hands. When anyone slipped, I reminded him or her with a single word: *"Hands!"*

I congratulated myself on having the situation pretty much under control, but Andrew continued to elude me. The words flew out of his mouth before he could think to get his hand up. Nothing I said seemed to make any impression upon his irrepressible nature. Suddenly I had an inspiration. I stopped on the staircase, took out my pad, and wrote:

> Dear Andrew:
> *When you want to show*
> *you understand,*
> *don't call out,*
> *just raise your hand.*
> Thanks in advance,
Ms. Lander

Halfway through my social studies lesson I asked the class about the causes of the Revolutionary War. Hands were waving all over the room and one voice called out, "Taxation without representation!" It was Andrew, of course. I walked over to his desk, smiled pleasantly at him, and handed him my folded note. He opened it, smiled back at me, and raised his hand for the rest of the period!

The next morning he said he had a poem for me. I read

it and asked him to write it on the board as a general reminder to the whole class. In large letters Andrew
printed:

> *Roses are red.*
> *Lettuce is green.*
> *If you raise your hand,*
> *it will be seen.*

I never had to say another word about not calling out
after that. I'd simply point to Andrew's poem.

ENGAGING COOPERATION
At Home and in School

Adult: Who's responsible for the mess on this floor?

Instead of giving the above answer:

1. DESCRIBE THE PROBLEM.
   "I see wet paint all over the floor."

2. GIVE INFORMATION.
   "It's easier to remove paint before it dries."

3. OFFER A CHOICE.
   "You can clean it up with a wet rag or a damp sponge."

4. SAY IT WITH A WORD OR GESTURE.
   "The paint!"

5. DESCRIBE WHAT YOU FEEL.
   "I don't like seeing the floor splattered with paint."

6. PUT IT IN WRITING.

ATTENTION ALL ARTISTS:
Kindly restore floor to original condition
before leaving the room.
> Thank you,
> The Management

7. BE PLAYFUL (USE ANOTHER VOICE OR ACCENT).
   In country-and-western style sing:

   > *Ah see paint thar on the floor,*
   > *An' it's a sight ah do deplore.*
   > *Git out your mop an' rags galore,*
   > *An' help to do this little chore.*

Questions and Stories from Parents and Teachers

Questions from Parents

1. Isn't how you say something as important as what you say?

Your tone of voice is easily as important as your words. The most skilled response can be toxic when delivered with a sigh of disgust that implies: "You've done it again. . . . You'll never learn." Along with our words of respect, we need an *attitude of respect*—one that signals, "I have confidence in your ability and your judgment. Once I point out the problem, you'll know what to do."

2. The other day my daughter came crying to me because one of her brothers had torn out some pages from her new notebook. I asked both boys who did it and they both denied it. How can I get them to tell the truth?

The question "Who did it?" sets off an instant alarm within children. They're now faced with two unpleasant alternatives. If they lie and get away with it, they'll have short-term relief but long-term guilt. If they tell the truth, they can expect a scolding or possibly a punishment. Worse yet, their confession may bring on an even more threatening question: "*Why* did you do it?"

No matter how a child tries to justify his actions, he feels the real answer to why he committed his "crime" is a litany of self-incrimination: "Because I'm dumb, mean, self-centered, inconsiderate, and thoughtless."

Rather than ask children *who* did what or *why* they did it, state the problem: "Suzie is very upset. Some pages were torn from her new notebook." Follow that with information: "If anyone in this family runs out of paper, ask me and I'll help you find some."

3. Whenever I want my daughter to do something, I try to ask her politely. I'll say, "Please hurry or you'll be late for school," or "Please turn off the TV and start your book report now," but she ignores me. What would you advise?

Adults often use "please" to soften the impact of a direct order. Children often tune out the "please" and rebel against the order. That, in turn, infuriates most parents. What is worse, some children use the "please formula" to make their own demands: "Mom, you have to take me to the store now, *please*. I said 'puhleeze,' didn't I?" Since there are so many other options for engaging cooperation (see the "Quick Reminder" on page 83), we suggest you save "please" for a situation in which you have little emotional investment and merely wish to model a common courtesy, for example, "Please pass the bread."

4. At what age do you recommend parents start writing notes to their children?

Surprisingly enough the written word can be very effective for children who are too young to read. A mother told us that her daughter took forever to get ready for preschool in the morning. One afternoon the mother sat down with her and listed all the things that had to be done before leaving the house. Next to the words for each task (brush teeth, comb hair, eat breakfast, etc.) she drew a simple picture. From then on the little girl consulted her list every morning to help herself get ready for school. Then one day she proudly covered the pictures with one hand and "read" her entire list to her daddy.

5. When my son carried on about how he wasn't going to "make a stupid speech" even if his teacher failed him, I told him that he had to and gave him a choice: He could practice it in front of his mirror or in front of me. He refused to do either. Any suggestions?

When a youngster has strong negative feelings about doing something, he can experience a choice as manipulation or entrapment. Before he can even begin to entertain the options you offer, he needs to know that you understand his resistance. For example, "The thought of standing up in front of an audience and giving a speech can be very scary. Even professionals get nervous! What do you think would make you feel more relaxed or confident? Practicing your talk in front of a mirror? . . . Trying it out on the family?"

Your choices might even lead your son to come up with a third option: "Maybe I'll say it into my tape recorder and play it back until I know it."

By being on his side and acknowledging the difficulty of his task, you make it possible for him to hear your choices and to consider them.

Stories from Parents

THIS FIRST EXAMPLE SHOWS A FATHER USING HIS NEW SKILLS TO help his teenage son live more cooperatively with a foreign exchange student who was spending the year with them.

My son, Jack, was doing his homework and listening to his favorite rock station. I could see that André, our foreign exchange student from France, was having a hard time concentrating on his homework but was too polite to say anything. He just kept looking in the direction of the radio. I was infuriated by my son's insensitivity. I was about to ask him how he expected André to work with all that noise, but then I thought that maybe I'd be better off just giving him information. I said, "Jack, some people can do homework with loud music. Others need quiet to be able to think." Jack looked up, turned the radio down slightly, and asked André, "Is this okay?"

About a half hour later, I heard the volume creeping up again. I poked my head into the boys' room and yelled, "The music!" Jack said, "Oh, sorry," and turned it off. André said, *"Merci."*

*   *   *

THIS STORY WAS FROM A MOTHER WHO SAID SHE RELIED HEAVILY upon play to engage the cooperation of her three-year-old daughter, Mindy.

Mindy was about to get into the wading pool with her library book. I was too far away to stop her, so I

87

yelled, "Oh, no! Book, stop! Book, you can't get in the pool. Books can't swim!" Mindy stopped in her tracks, looked at the book in her hand, and quickly ran it back to the house. A second later she was out again and into the pool.

*   *   *

THESE NEXT TWO STORIES ILLUSTRATE THE POWER OF THE WRITTEN word.

Andy, my ten-year-old, begged me to lend him my best casserole dish for the international food fair at school. When the fair was over, he neglected to bring it back. I reminded him every day for a week to bring it home, but he never did. Finally I took a felt marker and wrote "CASSEROLE!!" on the banana I packed for his lunch. Later that afternoon he told me all the kids laughed when he took out his banana. But he still forgot to bring the thing home!

I said, "Andy, this calls for strong measures. *You* need to write the kind of note to yourself that will get the job done." He sat right down and wrote:

> Dear Andy,
> Remember to bring home the stupid,
> stinky, smelly, dirty, dumb cazeroll
> tomorrow—or else!!!

I didn't correct his spelling. He taped the note on his book bag, and the next afternoon I had my casserole dish back.

* * *

MY DOG WAS AT THE WINDOW, BARKING. I LOOKED OUT and saw my children and the neighbors' children fighting at the bus stop—shouting and punching and kicking each other. I was still in my bathrobe so I quickly wrote "STOP FIGHTING!!" on a large piece of paper and tied it with a string to the dog's collar. Then I let her out hoping she would go to the children. She did, barking furiously. When the children saw the dog and read the note, they seemed stunned. They looked around, totally amazed. And they stopped fighting.

Questions from Teachers

1. What happens if I describe the problem and my student doesn't respond? The other day I said to my first grader, "Jim, your foot is in the aisle." He looked up, said, "Oh," and did nothing about it. I didn't know what to do after that.

You can always repeat your original statement. If that yields no results, go on to give information: "Someone could trip over it." Some children need to hear things more than once or in more than one way.

2. I'm wondering whether the idea of giving information works with teenagers. We were doing collage in my art class, and I said to one girl, "Sheila, paste dries out when it isn't covered." She rolled her eyes and said, "No kidding!" Why would she react like that?

Information needs to be age-appropriate. If you tell a teenager something she already knows, she experiences it as an insult to her intelligence. Sheila just needs the gentlest, swiftest reminder: "Sheila, the paste."

3. What's the difference between a one-word statement and giving a command? If I say, "Sit," isn't that the same as giving an order?

If you use a verb as your single word ("Stop!" . . . "Stand!" . . . "Move!" . . . "Sit!"), it will indeed sound like an order. A one-word statement works best when it's a noun. "Lori, your seat" causes Lori to think, "What about my seat? . . . Oh, I'm supposed to be in it. . . . I'd better sit down." You're not telling Lori what to do. You're directing her attention to the problem so that she can tell herself what to do.

4. I thought a choice was supposed to "engage co-operation." I have two girls in my class who never stop talking. I told them, "You have a choice: Either you stop that chattering or I'm changing your seats." Well, they didn't stop chattering, and when I finally did change their seats, they complained bit-terly that I was "unfair." What went wrong?

Your "choice" sounded too much like a threat. As soon as we say "Either you do this for me or I'll do that to you," the child will feel trapped and hostile.

Before offering an unappealing choice, it's a good idea to acknowledge your students' feelings. You could say something like "It's hard to sit near a good friend and not talk. There's so much you want to say to each other."

Then when you offer a choice, let it be one that makes the students feel you're on their side. "So, girls, what would be easier for you? To sit next to each other and restrain yourselves? . . . Or to change seats so you won't be tempted? Talk it over after school and tomorrow let me know what you've decided."

5. I think I could be comfortable expressing my real feelings to most of my students, and they probably would respond appropriately. But I have a few very tough customers in my class. Suppose I say, "It upsets me to see books on the floor," and one of them yells out, "Who cares?" What do I do then?

It may help if you tell yourself that your student's words are probably not aimed at you personally. Chances are he's either using you as a target for his displaced hostility or simply repeating in class what he hears at home. You can tell your tough customer, "I do. I care about how *I* feel. I care about how *you* feel. And I expect this to be a class where we *all* care about each other's feelings."

Stories from Teachers

A THIRD-GRADE TEACHER TOLD HOW HELPFUL IT WAS TO ONE OF her students when she gave him information instead of a scolding.

> Max came in before recess was over, looking agitated. I said, "Max, you seem upset."
>
> He said, "What's pro-puree?"
>
> I said, "Potpourri?"
>
> He said, "Yeah," and handed me a referral slip from the recess supervisor. "She yelled at me," he said, "because I wasn't being pro-puree."

I unfolded the referral slip and read it aloud: "*I caught this boy spitting on the playground. I am taking away his recess privileges today, because his behavior is not appropriate.*"

Max said, "See, she said I wasn't pro-puree. What is that?"

"What she wanted you to know," I explained, "is that what you did wasn't *appropriate*. That means that it's not okay to spit on the playground."

Max looked confused.

I said, "Max, spitting spreads germs."

He said, "Oh."

And that was it. He never did it again.

*   *   *

THE PRINCIPAL OF A PRIVATE SCHOOL TOLD WHAT HAPPENED when he acknowledged the feelings of a defiant student and offered him a choice.

As the principal I'm often called upon to play "the heavy." Yesterday one of my teachers sent a message to my office asking me to please come out and "do something" about Tommy, who refused to come in from recess. I wondered what in the world I could do short of carrying him in. When I came out, I saw Tommy hunkered down with a red-faced teacher standing over him yelling, "I told you I was going to call the principal."

I took a deep breath and said, "Hello, Tommy. Seems to me you're having a hard time leaving this playground. And no wonder. It's such a nice spring day." Tommy said nothing and continued to stare at the ground.

92

I said, "You probably wish you could stay out for the rest of the morning. . . . Well, son, it's time to get back to class now. So what do you say? Should we go in this door or that door?"

Tommy pointed to the door that was farthest away and said, "That one."

I extended my hand. He took it and we walked back into the building together. I don't know who was more surprised—me or the teacher.

* * *

A JUNIOR HIGH SCHOOL TEACHER REPORTED HOW SHE FOUND A way to tap into her students' spirit of play in order to teach a potentially dull subject.

My language arts class was bored with my lesson on linking verbs and frankly I was, too. When I went home, I knew I needed to think of some way to liven things up or I'd spend another day yelling at them to stop talking and pay attention. I fooled around with the idea of writing a rap song, but could only come up with the first two lines.

The next morning I told the kids what I'd done and recited my opening lines. Everyone became excited. We spent the rest of the period working on the lyrics and by the time the bell rang we had the whole song. The students left the room singing it; they taught it to their friends; they sang it on the bus coming to school the next day; and they all did astonishingly well on their tests. Here's the "Linking Verb Rap" written by the students of Section 72 in Welsh-Roanoke Junior High School in Louisiana:

Yo! I have a little somethin'
To teach to you.
It's the linking verb rap
And it's easy to do!
A linking verb connects
A subject with a noun
And if you've done it right,
You can turn it around.
An adjective *can be*
In the predicate part.
Know what you're doin',
Then you'll be smart!
Look very carefully
And you will see
Most of the verbs
Are forms of "be"

Am, is, are, was, were

These are the past
And present of the verb.

Learn "seem," "appear,"
And "become,"
Then you will know
That you are done!

* * *

THIS FINAL STORY WAS FROM A SIXTH-GRADE HOMEROOM teacher who told us how she used the written word to stop a child from being teased by her peers.

The day Sara was transferred to my class, I knew there was going to be a problem. The second she walked through the door with her sad, moon face and overweight body, Margie, the leader of the in-group, smirked and rolled her eyes at her faithful followers. They all tittered, and Sara's face turned flame red.

That was only the beginning. Later that week I received reports from the gym teacher that Margie didn't want Sara on her team because she was "too fat." I heard from the lunchroom aides that Margie called out, "Here comes the human garbage pail!" when Sara passed by with her tray. The home economics teacher told me that someone called Sara "the blob."

I was outraged. I knew that not only was Margie the instigator, but she was constantly egging on her sidekicks. I considered speaking to her directly but didn't trust myself not to say something I'd regret. Finally I decided to write to Margie.

It took me many drafts to get the tone I wanted. (In my early versions, I went on and on about how angered and disgusted I was by her cruelty.) Here's what I finally typed and gave to her:

Dear Margie,
I need your help. As you must have noticed, Sara has been "put down" and ridiculed every day since she was transferred to our class. School must be very difficult for her.

You may be wondering why I've chosen to write to you. It's because I've seen your leadership qualities and the respect your friends have for you. I'm guessing that if you made it clear to them that a *person's weight is not a measure of her worth,* the teasing and hurtful jokes would stop.

I know this letter asks a great deal of you, but I have confidence that somehow you'll find a way to make Sara's school day a happier experience.

> Sincerely,
> Ms. G.

Margie never referred to the letter. But over the next few days the smirks and snide remarks slowly came to a halt. One of the girls asked Sara if she wanted to help build scenery for the class play and Margie picked her to be on the volleyball team. Sara was thrilled. So was I.

The Pitfalls of Punishment: Alternatives That Lead to Self-Discipline

MARK STOMPED IN FROM RECESS YELLING AND SWINGING HIS FISTS. ONCE AGAIN A HEATED SOCCER GAME had set him off. He came at his teacher with a flood of accusations.

Mark: Jason cheats! They said it was my fault, but it wasn't! It was Jason's! He kicked the ball out . . . not me! Mrs. Kenner made me sit on the bench for fighting, but I didn't start it! Jason did! Now Tom won't let me play on his team! I hate this school!

Teacher: That's enough! I've just about had it with you, Mark! You wonder why nobody wants to play with you when you come in here acting like a crybaby. Kids don't want to play with people who blame their problems on everybody else!

Mark: But . . .

Teacher:	No buts! I don't want to hear it. I've had enough of your excuses.
Mark:	But I didn't . . .
Teacher:	I don't want to hear one more word out of you. Next recess you are going to sit in the kindergarten room and think about how to act your age.

I was that teacher.

As soon as the words left my mouth, I regretted them. I knew I should have been more patient. But I had spoken to Mark about his immature behavior many times before, and my "little talks" never seemed to do any good.

For the rest of the day I couldn't stop thinking about Mark. What had I hoped to accomplish with him? Did my punishment reduce his agitation? No. Did it open a line of communication between us? Obviously not. Did it help him to resolve his problem? Again, no. Mark wasn't going to learn how to play with kids his own age by sitting in a room full of kindergartners. Then what drove me to punish him?

That's what I asked Jane as we walked down the hall together to the faculty meeting. As she paused to consider my question, I answered it myself. "I was mad and frustrated didn't know how else to get through to him."

"There's something else," Jane said. "Punishment feels familiar. I don't know about you, but I grew up hearing 'If you do this once more, you'll be punished' or 'You're getting exactly what you deserve.'"

"And how about 'I'm doing this for your own good'?" I added.

Jane smiled ruefully. "That, too. It was the way grown-ups taught a child a lesson."

"Right. But, Jane, I can still remember how I felt when

I was a child and heard those words. I can assure you I didn't learn any 'lesson.' I didn't think about how I could do better in the future. I just remember feeling angry and having fantasies of revenge: 'I'll fix them. I'll get back at them. I'll do it again, only next time I won't get caught.' Now I'm the grown-up trying to teach Mark a lesson and he's probably having the same reactions I did."

"And if that's true," said Jane, "if punishment leaves kids feeling hostile and vengeful, why do we parents and teachers continue to do it?"

Ken caught up to us. "I heard that," he said cheerfully, holding open the door to the library, where our meeting was being held. "It's because there are thirty of them and one of us and if we didn't punish, they'd run all over us."

"Get serious, Ken," I said.

"I am serious. How else do you enforce the rules? Sometimes you have to punish kids to teach them a lesson."

We were back to that again! "But, Ken," I tried to explain as we walked over to a table in the corner, "if punishment teaches a lesson, what are students learning? When a child is punished verbally—'I want you to write "I must not cheat" a hundred times!'—he probably tells himself, 'I'm no good! I deserve to be punished.' "

"And," Jane chimed in, "when a child is punished physically—'The paddle in the principal's office will change your mind about fighting!'—he learns 'It's okay for you to hit me, but it's not okay for me to hit . . . until I'm the one in charge.' "

Ken looked at both of us coolly. "I give my students plenty of room," he said, "and as you know, I don't object to having fun. But there is such a thing as limits. If I hear profanity or back talk or see disruptive behavior, they get punished." Then without another word he reached up to the shelves behind our table, which held the professional books in our library, and pulled out a few of them. "Listen to this," he said as he thumbed through them quickly. "Here are the words of some of the top educators in the field today who share my philosophy:

> Punishment . . . is often rapidly effective in the treatment of harmful behaviors.[1]
> In lieu of the ineffectiveness of other tried alternatives, punishment . . . may be a better solution than others.[2]
> Not using punishment . . . withholds a potentially effective treatment.[3]

"Here," Ken said, sliding the books across the table. "See for yourself. All written recently."

"I don't care when they were written," Jane snorted. "The thinking is archaic. Besides, you've quoted these people out of context. And what's more, there's another school of thought of which you may not be aware that takes a very different position." Then she proceeded to pull four books from the shelf and started turning pages furiously.

"Jane," I said, "maybe you ought to wait until after the meeting."

[1]Johnny L. Matson and Thomas M. DiLorenzo, *Punishment and Its Alternatives: A New Perspective for Behavior Modification* (New York: Springer Publishing Co., 1984), p. 10.

[2]David A. Sabatino, Ann C. Sabatino, and Lester Mann, *Discipline and Behavioral Management: A Handbook of Tactics, Strategies, and Programs* (Rockville, Md.: Aspen Systems Corp., 1983), p. 12.

[3]John O. Cooper, Timothy E. Heron, and William L. Heward, *Applied Behavior Analysis* (Columbus, Ohio: Merrill Publishing Co., 1987), p. 412.

"It's okay," said Ken. "People are still coming in. Besides, I want to hear this."

"Here we go," Jane said. "These are the thoughts of some authorities who believe that punishment is *not* an effective form of discipline.

"Dr. Haim G. Ginott says:

> Punishment does not deter misconduct. It merely makes the offender more cautious in committing his crime, more adroit in concealing his traces, more skillful in escaping detection. When a child is punished he resolves to be more careful, not more honest and responsible.[4]

"Dr. Irwin A. Hyman says:

> The use of corporal punishment teaches children that violence is the way to solve problems. Research shows that this message is taught to those who inflict the pain, to those who receive it, and to those who witness it. It does not help children develop the internal controls that are necessary in a democracy.[5]

"Dr. Rudolf Dreikurs says:

> Today parents and teachers no longer can make the child behave. Reality demands that we apply new methods to influence and to motivate children to cooperate. Punishment such as spanking, slapping, humiliating, depriving, and generally putting children

[4]Haim G. Ginott, *Teacher and Child* (New York: Avon Books, 1970), p. 122.

[5]Irwin A. Hyman, *Reading, Writing, and the Hickory Stick* (Lexington, Ky.: Lexington Books, 1990), p. 200.

down are outdated and ineffective means of disciplining children.[6]

"Dr. Albert Bandura says:

Punishment can control misbehavior, but by itself it will not teach desirable behavior or even reduce the desire to misbehave."[7]

Ken shrugged and launched into a long counterargument, but all I could think about were the last words Jane had read: "Reduce the desire to misbehave."

That was exactly what I wanted to be able to do. I wanted to know how to reach inside my students and turn that "desire to misbehave" into a desire to behave appropriately. I wanted to avoid the terrible fallout of punishment and encourage the children to be inner-directed and self-disciplined. I wanted to find some effective alternatives to punishment.

As the guidance counselor distributed some new forms for us to fill out, I whispered to Jane, "Maybe instead of threatening to send Mark to kindergarten, I should have acknowledged how angry he was and, when he calmed down, helped him think about what else he could do when he felt he was being treated unfairly. He didn't deserve to be punished."

Ken leaned over and said, "But how about a student who does?"

He had me there. My thoughts turned to Amy, the girl who had the lead in the school play I was directing for

[6]Rudolf Dreikurs, Bernice Bronia Grunwald, and Floy C. Pepper, *Maintaining Sanity in the Classroom* (New York: Harper & Row, 1971), p. 117.
[7]Albert Bandura, "Human Agency in Social Cognitive Theory," *American Psychologist,* 44 (1989), pp. 1175–84.

parents' night. I had to admit she was one kid I itched to punish.

In the parking lot after the meeting I told Jane about Amy and how furious she'd made me, and how I had chosen her for the part because she was outstanding during tryouts but how at rehearsals she was obnoxious. "She'll do anything and everything to draw attention to herself— giggles, primps, fools around, and as far as learning her lines is concerned, forget it. That's for the peasants. 'Princess Amy' can't be bothered to bring her script. I think she believes she can learn her entire part at the last minute. And maybe she can, but I have this awful picture in my head of parents' night with Amy standing center stage, looking blank and glassy-eyed, and me in the wings feeding her lines in a loud stage whisper."

"What would you like to do to her?" Jane asked. "Give me your worst punishment fantasy."

"I can't. It's too mean."

"Indulge yourself."

"I'd like to sic Mrs. Kane on her."

"Who's she?"

"My fifth grade teacher. She was one tough cookie— never let anybody get away with anything."

"Okay, so what would Mrs. Kane do to Amy? Come on, Liz, at least you'll get it out of your system. Then we'll be very professional and see if we can figure out some reasonable alternatives."

On the following pages, in cartoon form, you'll see my punishment fantasy, and all the possibilities we considered using instead.

MY PUNISHMENT FANTASY

ALTERNATIVES TO PUNISHMENT

POINT OUT A WAY TO BE HELPFUL

Amy, it would be helpful if you used the time you're not on stage to study your lines.

EXPRESS STRONG DISAPPROVAL

I'm not pleased! It's not fair to the rest of the cast when one person is unprepared.

STATE YOUR EXPECTATIONS

I expect that when you say you'll learn your part, you'll be a person of your word.

SHOW HOW TO MAKE AMENDS

Here's what you can do to get back on track. Come to the next rehearsal with the entire first act memorized.

And if Amy still doesn't cooperate?

OFFER A CHOICE

But suppose Amy still makes no effort to learn her lines?

LET HER EXPERIENCE THE CONSEQUENCES OF HER BEHAVIOR

What actually happened? I never had to take that final drastic step. Just knowing that I had so many different options sent me back to the next rehearsal with a completely different attitude. There would be no blame or warnings or dire threats. When I took Amy aside and told her how I felt and described how she could get back on track, she listened quietly. At the next rehearsal I noticed a change in her behavior. By the end of the week she had learned all of her lines.

The following Monday at lunch I told Jane, Ken, and Maria about my small triumph.

Ken challenged me immediately. "But what if she *hadn't* learned her lines? What if you had to 'let her experience the consequences of her behavior' and dropped her from the cast? How different is that from punishment?"

I was taken aback by his questions. How could I find the words that would make clear to him what was just becoming clear to me? "It was my intent that was different," I said slowly. "My intent was not to hurt her or to deprive her or to get back at her. It wasn't even to 'teach her a lesson.' It was to protect the cast and to make sure that after all their work, they would have a reasonable shot at putting on a play they could feel proud of. And to protect me—from unnecessary stress."

Maria frowned. "Still, the girl would be mad at you," she said.

Jane came to my defense. "That's possible," she said, "but chances are she'd also be mad at herself. After the initial shock, she might say to herself, 'I'm very disappointed. . . . I really wanted that part. . . . If only I had learned my lines and not fooled around. . . . Next time I'm in a play, I'll be more serious and more prepared.' In other words, after doing her 'emotional homework,' the hope is that Amy would grow from the experience."

"Maybe you're right," Maria sighed, "but I don't know.

I'm having trouble with Marco right now, and I feel pulled to both sides. My husband believes that when children do something wrong, they should be punished. But I don't like to punish, even though my parents punished us when we were children."

"*Marco* is giving you trouble?" Ken asked incredulously. "That doesn't sound like him. He's such a great kid. The day he came to school with you before the term began, he helped me unpack all my books and set up my room."

"I know, he's a good boy," Maria said, "but he did a bad thing. The other day he took out his ruler and started a pretend sword fight in the hall with Jimmy, this boy in his class. My husband always warns Marco not to be so wild, to *think* before he acts, but Marco never listens, and as a result I got a call from the teacher and then from the principal."

"Just for horsing around?" Ken said.

"It was more serious than that. Jimmy's glasses got broken. Marco knocked them off and accidentally stepped on them. Then Jimmy's parents called my husband. They were very angry about the glasses. They said they were new and they paid a lot of money for them and it was Marco's fault for starting up."

"Well, that's another story," Ken said. "If my kid did that, I would've punished him, too. . . . So what do you say to that, Jane?"

"I think," said Jane, "that it's more important that we ask ourselves what Marco would say to himself if he were punished. And what Marco would say to himself if his parents tried to use an alternative to punishment."

We all talked a great deal after that, trying to project what would happen in each scenario. On the next two pages you'll see the essence of how we imagined the dialogue might go if Marco's parents punished him . . . and if they didn't.

PUNISHMENT

AN ALTERNATIVE TO PUNISHMENT

"Well, I have to admit there's a slight difference between the two approaches," Ken said.

"A *slight* difference!" Jane exclaimed. "In the first dialogue, where Marco is being punished, he's left feeling angry and helpless."

"And in the second dialogue," I said, "Marco still gets his parents' strong disapproval, but he's also expected to make amends. And he's left feeling like a basically good person who, even if he did do something wrong, could find a way to make it right."

Ken turned to Maria. "So what are you going to do?" he challenged her. "Has all this talk helped you make up your mind?"

Maria looked at him solemnly. "I know what I'm going to say to my husband tonight," she said quietly. "And I know what we're *both* going to say to Marco."

ALTERNATIVES TO PUNISHMENT
At Home and in School

Child: Oh !#!%!*!$!# I can't do this math!

Adult: I warned you over and over again not to use foul language. Now you're going to be punished.

Instead of giving the above answer:

1. POINT OUT A WAY TO BE HELPFUL.

"I hear your frustration. It would be helpful if you could express it without cursing."

2. EXPRESS YOUR STRONG DISAPPROVAL (WITHOUT ATTACKING CHARACTER).

"That kind of language upsets me."

3. STATE YOUR EXPECTATIONS.

"I expect you to find some other way to let me know how angry you are."

4. SHOW THE CHILD HOW TO MAKE AMENDS.

"What I'd like to see is a list of some strong words you could use instead of the ones you just did. Try the dictionary or thesaurus if you need help."

5. OFFER A CHOICE.

"You can curse to yourself—in your head—or you can use words that won't offend anyone."

(And if the child continues to use obscenities?)

6. LET THE CHILD EXPERIENCE THE CONSEQUENCES OF HIS BEHAVIOR.

"When I hear those words, I lose all desire to help you—with math or anything else."

Questions and Stories from Parents and Teachers

Questions from Parents

1. I've recently become a stepmother to two boys. My husband believes that if they fail a subject, they should have something deducted from their allowance. I think they should be given an increase in their allowance when they get good grades. Wouldn't rewarding them be a more positive way to get them to work harder?

Strange as it may seem, studies show that both rewards and punishment, in the long run, actually reduce the desire to learn.[8] Children learn best when they care about mastering a subject. A child who receives a good grade already has his reward. All he might want from his parents is an acknowledgment of their pleasure in his achievement. A child who receives a failing grade has already had a punishing experience. What he needs is a parent who will empathize with his feelings of discouragement and then go on to help him to figure out what went wrong and what to do about it.

---

[8]Alfie Kohn, *Punished by Rewards* (New York: Houghton Mifflin Publishing Co., 1993).

2. Whenever my daughter, Jill, comes home from preschool looking unhappy, I know it's because the teacher has sent her to the "time-out" chair. The other night I was angry at my husband and Jill said, "Daddy, I think you'd better go to time-out." I was surprised because that's not a method I use with her at home. Now I'm beginning to wonder if it should be used in school. What do you think?

Time-out has a very friendly, innocent sound. After all, the youngster isn't being hit or yelled at. She's just being stopped and removed from the scene. But even though some authorities in the field of child care recommend the method highly, the National Association for the Education of Young Children includes time-out in its list of harmful disciplinary measures—right along with physical punishment, criticizing, blaming, and shaming.

It's not hard to see why. As an adult you can imagine how resentful and humiliated you would feel if someone forced you into isolation for something you said or did. However, it may be more difficult to imagine what goes on inside a child who is sent to do "time" in a time-out chair. Nevertheless, try it. Put yourself in the shoes of a four- or five-year-old. Imagine that you are so angry at a little boy in your class named Jeffrey (who either shoved you or called you a name or grabbed something from you) that in retaliation you either kick him or hit him or swear at him or throw something at him. Now imagine two different responses to your antisocial action from your teacher:

In the first scenario the teacher says, "Stop that! That is not a nice thing to do. You need to go to time-out—right *now!*"

Chances are, as you slowly walk to your time-out chair, you might think: "The teacher isn't fair. She didn't see what Jeffrey did to *me*. It's all *his* fault." Or "Maybe I really *am* bad. So bad that I need to be sent away."

In the second scenario the teacher says to you, "You were so angry at Jeffrey that you kicked him. Kicking isn't allowed. Tell Jeffrey what you don't like *with words*. . . . And you can!"

Chances are this time you'd say to yourself, "My teacher understands why I was mad at Jeffrey. She won't let me kick him, but she thinks I can tell him what I feel with words. Maybe I can."

These are two very different sets of inner messages. The first convinces the child that there is something so wrong with her that she has to be removed from society; the second teaches her how to deal with society—assertively and nonviolently.

Does that mean that there is never a time for a child to be separated from the group? Some teachers believe that every classroom should have a haven a child can retreat to in times of stress. This "take-a-break place" or "cool-off corner" can be equipped with some books, drawing materials, and pillows to punch or lie on. It's important that the child not be ordered to go there. Instead the teacher could offer her a choice so that the youngster herself can determine whether or not she should go: "I can see you're still angry at Jeffrey. Do you want to tell me more about it or do you want to use the paper and crayons in the cool-off corner to draw how you feel?"

3. For someone like me, with my temper, not spanking my son, but giving him time-out instead, is a big step forward. What else can you do when you feel you're about to lose control?

One mother reported that she gives herself time-out when she is about to "blow." She said, "When I saw my son mindlessly making scratch marks on the dining room table with the point of his new compass, I grabbed it away from him and said, 'I'm so angry at what I see, I'm going to my room to cool off!' " Later when she calmed down, she showed her chastened son how to repair the damage.

When Dr. Haim Ginott was challenged by a parent as to what he'd do if he were "pushed over the edge," he drew himself up to his full height, glared at an imaginary little offender, raised his right arm in a threatening gesture, and bellowed, "I am so angry, I'm about to hit! . . . *So run for your life!!"*

4. My son's teacher kept all the boys after school yesterday because the security guard told her that some of her students were smoking in the boys' bathroom. As a result my son missed basketball practice and was very upset. He thinks group punishments are unfair. What do you think?

It's not hard to understand your son's objection to group punishment. Innocent students resent it deeply and may conclude, "Why bother to follow the rules if I get punished anyway?" Those who are guilty may conclude, "I didn't get caught this time. Maybe I can get away with it again." If a teacher's goal is to help her students become self-disciplined, then punishment—group or individual—is not the answer.

5. My school district is in favor of corporal punishment and state law still allows it. Several parents, including myself, are concerned that slapping or spanking children is harmful; however, we don't know if it's possible to build a case against physical punishment in our school. Where can we find support for our point of view?

You are not alone in your concerns. The following is only a partial list of organizations that favor outlawing corporal punishment in schools:

American Academy of Pediatrics
American Bar Association
American Medical Association
American Psychological Association
Child Welfare League of America
NAACP
National PTA
National Committee for the Prevention of Child Abuse
National Association of School Psychologists
National Mental Health Association

Among the long list of countries that do not allow teachers to hit schoolchildren are England, Poland, Italy, Russia, China, France, Germany, Spain, the Scandinavian countries, Israel, Turkey, and Japan.

The National Center for the Study of Corporal Punishment and Alternatives in the Schools in Pennsylvania gives information and support to those who seek it. Their goal is to add the United States to the list of countries that have abolished corporal punishment.

THIS FIRST EXPERIENCE WAS FROM THE MOTHER OF NINE-YEAR-old Megan.

I came home from work at two o'clock one afternoon because I didn't feel well. Imagine my shock when I heard children's laughter coming from my daughter's bedroom. I ran upstairs and there was Megan and her friend JoAnn. They stopped laughing as soon as they saw me and looked at each other guiltily. I had a hard time getting it out of them, but they finally admitted that they came home for lunch and never returned to school.

I said, "You mean you cut school."

JoAnn said, "But we didn't do it on purpose. We were talking and we forgot to look at the clock."

I told JoAnn she'd better go home because I needed to speak to Megan privately. When her friend left, I said to Megan, very quietly, "You didn't forget to look at the clock."

Megan lowered her head and said, "We were just experimenting to see what it would feel like not to go back to school."

For the moment I didn't know what to do. I considered punishing her—telling her she couldn't have JoAnn over for the next month. But instead I said, "I'm very upset by all this. When you're supposed to be in school, that's where I expect you to be. Now I'm probably going to get a phone call from your teacher."

Megan said, "Write me an absence note. Say I was sick and then you won't get a call."

119

I said, "Megan, the note has to come from you and it has to be the truth." Well, she wasn't very happy about that, but she did write a note (with a little help from me) saying she was just "experimenting" and that she wouldn't do it again.

Afterward I felt good. I was firm, I didn't "get crazy," and even though it turned out that the teacher gave her a hard time over the note, I still felt I did the right thing. I knew I had helped Megan face up to what she did and take responsibility.

*   *   *

THIS NEXT STORY WAS FROM A PARENT OF A HIGH SCHOOL student.

My sixteen-year-old daughter, Carol, told me she was studying child development in her home economics class, and one day the teacher asked, "What do you think would happen to a child if he or she were never punished?" When Carol told the class that she had never been hit or punished by her parents, the other students looked at her with their mouths open. One of the girls said, "But . . . but . . . you're good!"

I guess they couldn't believe that someone could turn out to be "good" without having been punished. I suppose if children were raised with spankings and punishments, it would be hard for them to understand that when parents trust kids and talk to them respectfully, the kids can end up being very "good" and very responsible people. To me Carol is living proof of that.

Only last week my husband and I returned from

an evening out and found a note from her on our pillow. It said:

> Dear Mom and Dad,
> Tonight while backing out of the driveway I hit the oak tree and dented the fender of your car. Enclosed is ten dollars—the first payment to cover the cost of repairs. Each month I'll pay a similar amount until it's all paid for. I'm really sorry!! It was an accident.
> Love,
> Carol

I must admit we were a little angry at first, but after we cooled down, we were kind of proud.

*   *   *

THIS NEXT EXPERIENCE WAS REPORTED BY A FATHER.

The superintendent called a meeting of all the parents to discuss the alarming increase in drug use in the district. A panel of mental health professionals addressed us and they were all excellent, but the speaker who really got through to me was a dropout from our high school who had just been through a drug rehabilitation program. She told us about her alcoholic father who was never there for her, her mother who remarried and stopped paying attention to her, her long history of getting into trouble in school, acting tough, turning to drugs, and eventually living in the street and being terrified of getting AIDS, as a few of her friends had.

At the end of her story, she looked around the room and said:

> All I can say to you is please, listen to your children. I really think if my mom had listened to me more, instead of punishing me, I might have been able to listen to her. But instead, I just got angry about always being grounded and would defy her by sneaking out my bedroom window. If she'd been more my friend and less a punishing parent, it might have made a difference. All a kid's really got is her family. In the end that's who's there for you. But you parents should listen more and judge less, so we can talk to you better.

Questions from Teachers

1. I've taught in many schools and have witnessed all kinds of punitive practices, from sarcasm and ridicule to threats of detention or suspension. Some teachers deprive kids of what they enjoy most—sports, music, trips, etc. Others use a more physical approach. They'll slap, shake, pinch, or pull hair. Of all these practices, which would you say was the most harmful?

In his book *Reading, Writing, and the Hickory Stick*, Dr. Irwin Hyman says that all of these punitive practices can leave a child with serious long-term aftereffects. His research shows that even one harsh experience can cause a variety of posttraumatic stress symptoms: The child may lose interest in schoolwork, stop doing homework, and start behaving aggressively. He may experience feelings of anxiety or depression, or a loss of trust in adults. Some children start bed-wetting, nail biting, or stuttering, or suddenly develop headaches or stomachaches. Some experience nightmares or have trouble falling or staying asleep. Although one child might not experience all of these symptoms, no child should have to suffer any of them. Our children are entitled—if not by national law, then by a higher law—to be treated in humane and caring ways by those who claim the privilege of educating them.

2. I still can't accept the idea that there aren't some situations that call for punishment. How about a bully in the playground who grabs the glasses off a first grader, reduces him to tears, and laughs gleefully? Doesn't a child who behaves so cruelly deserve to be paddled?

He needs to be stopped and redirected. He doesn't need another demonstration of how bigger, stronger people can hurt smaller, weaker people. Chances are the "bully" knows that all too well from personal experience. If we wish to teach kindness, we must use methods that are kind. A child who is cruel to another child needs to experience the strength of your convictions, not the pain of a paddle. He needs to hear a stern "I don't like what I see!! No one should be teased to tears—ever!" He needs to hear your expectations of him: "I expect kindness from you . . . And you can start right now—by returning the glasses." Respect for others can only be taught respectfully.

3. Are you suggesting that any student can be "turned around" by relating to him respectfully?

Would that it were so! Sad to say, there are some children who have been so brutalized that they're unable to respond to caring ways. The short school day cannot begin to heal the long-term damage they have endured. The best that teachers can do is to protect the other students and themselves from these out-of-control children. However, it is especially important to use firm but respectful methods with these angry youngsters so as not to further enrage them. At the very least, everyone will be safer and no greater damage will have been done.

4. When I was on lunchroom duty, two girls got into a fistfight. The security guard wanted to bring them to the principal's office, but I told him I'd handle it myself. Each girl tried to tell me her side. I refused to listen and warned them that if it ever happened again, I'd personally take them to the principal. Now I'm having second thoughts. How else could I have handled it?

You could have listened as each girl stated her case, and then reflected each one's point of view: "So, Ellen, *you* were angry at Rosa because . . . And, Rosa, *you* were furious because *you* thought . . . " By acknowledging their rage at each other, you would have helped to defuse it.

A principal reported that whenever two children who had been fighting were brought to his office, he used a method he learned from the late child psychologist Dr. Haim Ginott. He would sit the students down at opposite ends of his desk, hand each of them a sharp pencil and a yellow legal pad, and say, "I want to know exactly what happened—in writing."

Typically, one of the antagonists would protest, "But it wasn't my fault." The other would counter with "He hit me first." The principal would nod and say, "Make sure you put that in your report. I want to know—in detail—

how it started, how it developed, and what each of you felt. And be sure to include your recommendations for the future!"

After the children finished writing, he would read both reports and respectfully acknowledge each child's experience. Then he'd ask them to share their recommendations with each other and come to an agreement.

Stories from Teachers

THIS FIRST STORY WAS FROM A JUNIOR HIGH SCHOOL TEACHER.

I came into my classroom and caught Joe drawing an elaborate picture on the inside cover of his math book. This was one day after I had given the class a lecture on not defacing school property.

Normally I would have yanked him out of his seat and yelled, "That's it! Go to the office!" Instead I walked over to his desk and stood there. Joe slammed his book shut, trying to hide his drawing. I said, "Let me repeat what I said yesterday: It makes me angry to see people marking up books. These textbooks are going to have to be used for the next five years, and I expect my students to take good care of them."

"Sorry," Joe mumbled. "I forgot."

"I see," I said, and went back to my desk. When I returned to Joe's desk a moment later, he was diligently trying to erase the drawing with his tiny, worn-out eraser. I handed him mine and said, "Here, this might make the job easier. And you can use this small pad whenever you get the urge to doodle." Joe looked surprised and said, "Thanks."

I said, "You're welcome," and started my lesson.

A month has passed, and Joe hasn't drawn in his textbook since. He keeps the pad in his shirt pocket and shows me his drawings from time to time. I'm glad I didn't send him to the office that day. It might have stopped him from marking up his books, but we never would have had the relationship we have today. And who knows, I may have encouraged a budding Picasso.

*   *   *

A GUIDANCE COUNSELOR REPORTED HOW SHE HELPED A CHILD avoid his teacher's threatened punishment by accepting his feelings and offering him a choice.

I went into a third-grade classroom to pick up three children to be tested for a special education program. Two of them got up immediately to come with me. Khalil just sat there, head down, looking angry. The classroom teacher said, "Khalil, Ms. Gordon is here. She's waiting. [No response.] Well, I can see Khalil doesn't want to be cooperative today. [Still no response.] Khalil, if you want to go on that field trip tomorrow, you'd better leave with Ms. Gordon now." Khalil's head sank lower. I went over to his seat, knelt down beside him, and whispered, "You don't want to come today."

Khalil (angrily): I don't want to be near Joseph!

Me: Oh . . . Well, I can think of two possibilities: You can come with me and I'll keep Joseph as far away from you as possible . . . or I can give you the test now, right here in this classroom.

Khalil was quiet for a long time. Then he got up and left with me. I was so glad I was able to think of a choice that would give him a way out.

*   *   *

Sean was seven—an attractive, intelligent child in a class for children with emotional and behavioral difficulties. He did poorly in school and no amount of encouragement, gold stars, or stickers made much of a dent in his defenses. He averted his gaze from those who wished to help him, shrugged his shoulders when asked what the trouble was, and at home slithered away from his mother's affectionate overtures. He also feared heights. No slides or jungle gyms for him.

History given by the family revealed that Sean's early discipline in school had included the paddle in first grade for inattention and a ruler on his shoulder blades and knuckles in the second grade for disruptive behavior. His mother, meaning to be cooperative with the school, had given the teacher permission, in Sean's presence, to handle him however she thought best.

I encouraged the parents to talk about these matters with Sean in relaxed, informal sessions. They were surprised after only one or two times to find Sean clearly recalling each school experience of being paddled or struck with a ruler. Suddenly he blurted out to his mother his first expression of pent-up rage as he beat his fists on her knee: "But,

127

Mom, you told her she could hit me. You told her she could!"

His mother was taken aback. She explained that she never intended to have anyone hurt him. At the end of the session she and Sean shared an affectionate hug for the first time in over a year.

A day or so later Sean and his father were playing outside with a ball that became stuck on the roof of the house. The father took out the ladder, intending to go after the ball, but Sean suddenly said, "No, let me." He successfully negotiated the ladder and retrieved the ball—obviously overjoyed with himself. He ran into the house, grabbed his mother around the waist, and shouted triumphantly, "Mom, since I told you my secret, I can do anything!"

Needless to say, his schoolwork improved markedly from then on.

4

Solving Problems Together: Six Steps That Engage Children's Creativity and Commitment

ON THE LAST DAY OF MY FIRST YEAR OF TEACHING, TASHA, A CHRONIC TALKER WITH A LOUD VOICE, TOLD me, "You were too easy on us. You let us get away with murder."

I laughed and said, "Why didn't you tell me this sooner?"

She answered, "I was having too much fun!"

We both smiled as she sauntered out the door, but as soon as she was gone, my smile vanished. Could Tasha be right? Had I let the kids get away with murder? Maybe. I was so eager not to be punitive, to be liked by everyone, that I overlooked what I considered petty stuff—kids interrupting each other or putting each other down or someone shouting across the room. Why spoil an interesting lesson by making a big deal over a few minor transgressions? But Tasha had let me know that she had taken advantage of my desire to be "nice." And she probably wasn't the only one.

I resolved to be tougher next year—to lay down the rules on the first day of class and to be strict about enforcing them. But after a few weeks into September I found myself slipping again. For instance, my idea of a good discussion is a lively, free-flowing exchange with one thought sparking another. If one student excitedly interrupted another, that didn't seem like a cardinal sin to me. If someone disagreed with what she heard, and in the heat of the moment sneered, "That's stupid," I let it go. But as the interruptions and put-downs grew, our class discussions rapidly degenerated into noisy brawls.

Still, I couldn't bring myself to dampen the enthusiasm with reminders and reprimands. Maybe I was naive, but my expectation was that at some point the kids themselves would realize that they should start being more civil to each other. The only realization that came was mine. These kids weren't about to change unless their teacher changed. They needed an adult to teach them some basic social skills and to insist that they use them. But how would I go about it?

I thought about the chapter on problem solving in *How to Talk So Kids Will Listen*. . . . The theory is that when parents and children examine problems and work out solutions together, children are much more likely to try to make those solutions work.

An interesting idea. I studied the step-by-step process for problem solving and wrote out my own adaptation for possible use with my class.

- Listen to my students' feelings and needs.
- Summarize their point of view.
- Express my feelings and needs.
- Invite the class to brainstorm with me to find a solution.

- Write down all ideas—without evaluating.
- Together decide which ideas we plan to use and how we plan to implement them.

As I reviewed the six steps, I felt momentarily over-whelmed. Could I actually steer the class through this whole long, complicated process? Then again, maybe it wouldn't be as hard as it seemed. "Basically," I told my-self, "it's a matter of the kids expressing their feelings, of me expressing mine, and then all of us working together on finding solutions." Certainly it was worth a try. Here, in cartoon form, are the highlights of what took place the first time I tried problem solving with my students:

PROBLEM SOLVING

LISTEN TO YOUR STUDENTS' FEELINGS AND NEEDS

SUMMARIZE THEIR POINT OF VIEW

EXPRESS YOUR FEELINGS AND NEEDS

INVITE THE CLASS TO BRAINSTORM WITH YOU TO FIND A SOLUTION

WRITE DOWN ALL IDEAS—WITHOUT EVALUATING

TOGETHER DECIDE WHICH IDEAS YOU DON'T LIKE, WHICH YOU DO, AND HOW YOU PLAN TO PUT THEM INTO ACTION

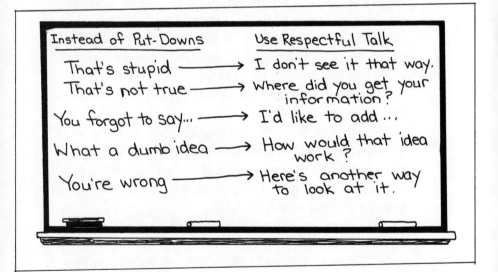

Important changes took place as a result of that problem-solving session. The number of interruptions dropped dramatically. Those few students who continued to interrupt would catch themselves and say, "Oops," or "Sorry," and then politely wait their turn. But the most gratifying outcome for me was the respectful way the kids began to listen to each other. Even those who slipped back into an unthinking "That's stupid!" were stopped in their tracks by a class groan. Typically, the offender would give an embarrassed smile, look at the board, and mechanically read, "I don't see it that way." Everyone would laugh, but even though it was a rote recitation, the new words changed the tone of the discussion. Best of all, I didn't have to worry about being the "put-down policeman." My students were in charge of monitoring themselves.

I was so proud of their new self-control and growing sensitivity to one another that on "Meet the Teacher" night I decided to tell the parents about it. After everyone was seated, I greeted the parents and shared my goals for the term. Then, pointing to the "Use Respectful Talk" chart on the chalkboard, I described the problem the class had had and the process we used to resolve it.

The parents seemed interested. A flurry of comments and questions followed:

"I just came back from a management training workshop and the conflict resolution skills they taught us were very much like the ones you just described."

"This sounds like the kind of thing you could do at home with your own kids."

"I'd never have the patience to go through all those steps with my children."

"Suppose a child isn't willing to think about solutions?"

"Or suppose he comes up with an idea that's foolish or dangerous, then what do you do?"

"What happens if you agree to a plan and the kids don't hold up their part of the bargain? Then what?"

Clearly they all wanted to know more. I explained that I had no experience using these methods as a parent but that, if they were interested, I'd be glad to share what I had discovered as a teacher. They were very interested. I started by explaining that the more I experimented with the problem-solving approach, the more I realized how much I had to keep in mind in order to make it work. Here are the highlights of what I told the parents I had learned from trial and error:

Don't even try to problem solve if you're feeling rushed or agitated. In order to tackle a difficult problem successfully, you need time, a clear head, and inner calm.

The first step—hearing the children out—is the most important. My tendency was to rush through this beginning step in order to get to the "good part," namely, brainstorming for as many solutions as possible:

Student:	Ms. Lander, I got a D on my social studies test!
Me:	Well, what can you do to make sure that doesn't happen again? Any ideas?

I've since learned that students are not willing to work on finding solutions until their feelings have been acknowledged:

Me:	You sound pretty upset about that grade. Let's go over your essay answers together. Maybe you can tell me more about what you had in mind.

Be brief when expressing your feelings. The kids could listen attentively to a short statement of what I felt, but they'd tune me out if I went on and on about *my* worry or *my* frustration or *my* resentment.

Resist the urge to evaluate their suggestions. It was very hard for me to keep myself from commenting when the kids came up with solutions that were clearly "off the wall." The time I said, "There is no way we could do that," was the time the whole problem-solving process screeched to a halt. No one offered a single suggestion after that. If you want to get the wheels of creativity spinning, you have to welcome every idea—no matter how nutty: "Okay, anyone who interrupts has to have his mouth taped up for a week. I've got that down. What else?"

Make sure to work out a plan to implement the final decision. I had to learn not to let myself relax in the glow of having helped to facilitate a wonderful solution. The best of intentions can go down the drain unless everyone agrees on a method for putting the solution into action and then deciding who will be responsible for what.

Don't lose heart if the plan fails. It's easy to berate the kids for not following through on their own plan. The one time I did, the class became sullen and hostile. I finally learned that it was much wiser to schedule another meeting and figure out what went wrong and how to fix it. In other words, one problem-solving session might not be enough. By returning to the drawing board you can usually find answers you missed the first time around.

At the end of my long monologue the bell rang. Some parents left to meet other teachers, but a few remained behind and clustered around my desk. They wanted a chance to talk more.

A father asked, "Do you think this method you just described could help with homework problems?"

"I'd be interested in your answer to that one," a mother said, "because from the time Lara comes home from school, I'm busy with her homework."

Her comment confused me. "*You're* busy with *her* homework?" I asked.

"Not all the time," she said, "but isn't a parent supposed to help with homework?"

"What kind of help?" I asked.

"Well . . . when Lara comes home from school, I make her show me her assignments and I go over them with her and help her get organized. This afternoon I took her to the library and we picked out some excellent books for her report on Eleanor Roosevelt."

I was horrified. Lara was a reasonably capable student. The purpose of my homework assignments was to give her and the other children a chance to organize their own time, to work independently, to exercise their own judgment. As tactfully as I could, I said, "It seems to me that the best kind of help we can give children is indirect help. Provide a quiet place to work, a good light, a dictionary, a snack if they're hungry, and just be available if they want to ask you something."

Lara's mother looked at me with raised eyebrows. Obviously my little speech hadn't convinced her of anything. I tried to recall what my parents had done with me and my sister when we were growing up. Homework was considered serious business in our house, a top priority. We had this routine where every night after dinner we cleared the kitchen table, sat down, spread out our books and papers, and did our homework. There was no question of whether we could or should or would do it. It was simply "homework time."

Aloud I said, "How would you feel about establishing a nightly routine with Lara? She could either work alone in her room or maybe somewhere near you, and little by little you could make yourself scarce and let Lara take over."

"I wish it were that simple," Lara's mother said with some irritation, "but the plain fact is, she won't do her homework if I don't keep after her. She—"

"Please don't take offense," another woman interrupted, "but I don't think you're being fair to your daughter. My mother used to hound me about my homework every night and hover over me to make sure that I did it all and got it right. Sometimes she'd take over and do it for me. After a while I wouldn't even start my homework unless my mother was there. I guess on some level I figured that as long as she was being responsible for me, I didn't have to be responsible for myself. So that's my reason for having a 'hands-off' homework policy with my daughter."

Lara's mother looked bewildered. "You mean you *never* help your child with her homework?"

"Well, if she's stuck, I'll listen to what's bothering her and try to get her unstuck. But the second she gets going again, I bow out. I want her to know that *she's* the one in charge of her homework and that she's basically capable of doing it herself."

"That's assuming she is," Lara's mother persisted. "But what if she isn't?"

Without hesitating the woman retorted, "Then get outside help—a tutor, a high school student—or tell her to call another kid in her class. Anything to avoid what happens when parents take over and become 'passionate' about their children's homework."

A man who had been listening intently nodded his head vigorously in agreement.

"What are you thinking?" I asked him.

"About my own father," he said. "It killed him that I was

140

having so much trouble with math. Finally he decided that *he* was the one to teach it to me. Every night he'd make me sit with him and listen to his long explanations. He'd always start out patiently, but when I still didn't get it, he'd become furious with me and explain it all again—only louder. I may have learned a little math from him, but it sure didn't do much for our relationship. That's why I make it clear to my son, Tim, that homework is his job, just the way my work is my job."

Another father challenged him. "But suppose Tim doesn't see it your way?"

"Well, as a matter of fact, last year he did give me a hard time. When Tim joined the soccer team, it became the most important thing in his life and I received a letter from his teacher saying that he hadn't been doing his homework."

"What did you say to him?" Lara's mother asked.

"Actually I didn't say anything to Tim. I made an appointment with the teacher for a conference. I thanked her for notifying me but told her that, knowing Tim, it would be far more effective if he received a letter from her instead of a lecture from me. Then I handed her five copies of a typed form that read:

Dear Tim,
The following assignments are still due:
Dates: _____

_____

Please let me know by tomorrow morning
when I can expect them.

                                 Sincerely yours,

"I also gave her five stamped, addressed envelopes and told her how much I appreciated her help."

We all looked at him expectantly. "Then what happened?" I asked.

"The first letter surprised him, but he managed to ignore it. But when the second one arrived and Tim realized that his teacher meant business, he started bringing in his homework. And he has ever since."

"My goodness," Lara's mother said with admiration, "you really solved that one!"

"Yeah, that worked out well, but this term I have another problem. Now he leaves his homework for the last minute and stays up until all hours trying to get it done. I'm always after him to start earlier and he always has some excuse why he can't. His sister is bothering him or he's working on his model airplanes or he's watching his TV show."

Lara's mother turned to me. "Ms. Lander, you were telling us about problem solving before. Do you see that approach as something that could work with Tim?"

"It might," I said, suddenly wishing Jane were here to help me.

Tim's father frowned. "Exactly how would you go about doing it?" he asked.

All eyes were on me. I asked Tim's father to describe what usually happened when he insisted that his son start his homework earlier. Then we all discussed what might happen if Tim and his father sat down and problem solved together. On the following pages you'll see the two scenarios we envisioned.

A BATTLE OVER HOMEWORK

SOLVING THE PROBLEM TOGETHER

LISTEN TO THE CHILD'S FEELINGS AND NEEDS

SHOW YOU UNDERSTAND

EXPRESS YOUR FEELINGS AND NEEDS

INVITE THE CHILD TO BRAINSTORM WITH YOU

WRITE DOWN ALL IDEAS—WITHOUT EVALUATING

Our Ideas

1. Stop bugging me.   (Tim)

2. Do all your homework as soon as you get home. (Dad)

3. Put the baby to bed earlier and I'll start my homework then. (Tim)

4. Break up the homework. Do the easy part when you get home and the hard part later. (Dad)

5. Keep Patti away from me when I'm working. (Tim)

6. Make up a schedule for work time, play time and bed time that you think you can stick to. (Dad)

TOGETHER DECIDE WHICH IDEAS YOU DON'T LIKE, WHICH YOU DO, AND HOW YOU PLAN TO FOLLOW THROUGH

A few days after "Meet the Teacher" night I had a call from Tim's father. He wanted to tell me what happened when he talked to his son. "It was pretty close to what we had imagined," he said. "The only problem was the schedule Tim worked out. He had himself watching *two* hours of TV and going to bed at eleven. I told him I wasn't comfortable with that. So we reviewed his schedule and I helped him revise it. We finally agreed that he'd start his homework a half hour earlier, allow *one* hour for TV, and be in bed by nine-thirty with lights out at ten o'clock."

As the weeks went by, my understanding and appreciation of the problem-solving approach continued to deepen. I began to see that the long-term benefits of the process were much greater than the immediate rewards of smoother classroom routines or the resolution of persistent problems at home. When we invite a child to join us in tackling a problem, we send a powerful set of messages:

"I believe in you."

"I trust your ability to think wisely and creatively."

"I value your contributions."

"I see our relationship not as 'all-powerful grown-up' exercising authority over 'ignorant child' but as adult and child who are equal, not in competence, not in experience, but equal in dignity."

If there's one thing we can guarantee all of our children, now and in the future, it's problems—sometimes one right after the other. But by teaching them how to approach a problem, by showing them how to break it down into manageable parts, by encouraging them to use their own ingenuity to resolve their problems, we are giving them skills they can depend upon for the rest of their lives.

PROBLEM SOLVING
At Home and in School

1. LISTEN TO THE CHILD'S FEELINGS AND NEEDS.

   Adult: You seem very upset about failing your Spanish test.

   Child: I am! I only got twelve words right out of twenty, and I studied for an hour last night!

2. SUMMARIZE THE CHILD'S POINT OF VIEW.

   Adult: You sound pretty discouraged. Even though you tried to cram all those new words into your head, some of them refused to stick.

3. EXPRESS YOUR FEELINGS AND NEEDS.

   Adult: My concern is that if you don't memorize the basic vocabulary, you'll get further and further behind.

4. INVITE THE CHILD TO BRAINSTORM WITH YOU.

   Adult: I wonder, if we put our heads together, could we come up with some new and more effective ways to study?

5. WRITE DOWN ALL IDEAS—WITHOUT EVALUATING.

   Child: Drop Spanish.

   Adult (writing): I've got that. What else?

   Child: Maybe I could . . .

6. TOGETHER DECIDE WHICH IDEAS YOU DON'T LIKE, WHICH YOU DO, AND HOW YOU PLAN TO PUT THEM INTO ACTION.

   Adult: What do you think of the idea of making flash cards and studying only four new words each night?

   Child: That's okay. But instead of flash cards, I like the idea of saying my words into a tape recorder and testing myself until I know them.

Questions and Stories from Parents and Teachers

Questions from Parents

1. I notice that you start problem solving by listening to the child's point of view. Would there be anything wrong with reversing the order and having the adult express what bothers her first?

That might work. However, some children become defensive and shut down when grown-ups begin by expressing their irritation. It's a lot easier for children to understand and care about an adult's point of view *after* the adult has demonstrated *genuine caring and acceptance of their feelings.*

2. I start problem solving with my kids with the best of intentions, but when I get to the part where I express my feelings, I find it hard not to start blaming and accusing them. Any ideas?

One way to avoid blame is to shun the accusing *you.* "*You* kids never ... *You* always ... The trouble with *you* is ..." Instead substitute an *I* for a *you.* For example, "Here's what *I* feel. *I* get upset when ... What *I'd* like to see is ..." As long as they're not being attacked, children can listen to your feelings without becoming defensive.

3. I noticed that sometimes when I start brainstorming with my children, they'll accuse me. For instance, I'll suggest, "Maybe I could do thus and so" and they'll say, "No, you won't. Remember last

time how you . . ." and suddenly we're sidetracked into a long argument about what happened in the past. Is there any way to avoid this?

If your children start to accuse you, you can get them back on track with a statement like "Let's not blame each other for what happened in the past. What we all need to think about now is a solution for the future."

4. I have a situation that can't be solved by problem solving. Hardly a week goes by that one or another of my three foster children doesn't tell me that someone at school either bullied him or called him a name or made fun of him because of his sneakers, his haircut, or the slant of his eyes. I tell them all to ignore that stupid nonsense. What else can I do?

A hurt should never be ignored. A wounded child needs to know that someone can understand his pain. He needs an adult to acknowledge how frightening or deeply hurtful it can be to be assaulted—either physically or emotionally, for any reason.

After you have given him your report, you can enlist the support of the other children. At a family meeting you can tackle the problem together. Everyone can discuss any or all of the following questions:

- Did anything like what happened to Chul Su ever happen to you? What was your reaction?
- What can you do when someone makes fun of you? Pretend you don't hear? Change the subject? Agree? Use humor? ("Yeah, it's a flat-top haircut. Makes it easier to stand on my head.")
- What can you do if you're physically threatened? Call for help? Yell, "Watch out behind

you!" and run away fast? Tell the bully you have a contagious, fatal disease? Learn karate?

- Who are the adults who can help put an end to the teasing or bullying? The teacher? The principal? Your foster parent? The "bully's" parent?

After you've written down all of the solutions that have come out of your discussion, the children can take turns practicing them by role-playing scenes in which one child teases or bullies another. By the end of your group problem-solving session, the children might all feel more empowered—as individuals and as a family.

 **Stories from Parents**

THIS FIRST STORY WAS FROM A MOTHER WHO USED PROBLEM solving as a way of taking the pressure off herself and helping her children become more responsible.

Last year my three girls (six, eight, and twelve) carried on so much about having to have the "right" clothes and the "right" sneakers and the "right" supplies for the new school year that I let them steamroller me into spending more than I could afford.

This year when the first back-to-school ads came out in the paper, I decided to head the kids off at the pass. I called a family meeting and asked them to write down all the things they felt they absolutely had to have for the new term. (We also made up a "wish list" for what they'd like to buy if the family won the lottery.) Then I told them, in plain language, about my need to exercise a little fiscal restraint so that we could continue to enjoy the basic necessities of life—like eating and having a roof over our heads.

They protested at first but after a while started coming up with all kinds of suggestions—everything from "We'll bake cookies and sell them to the neighbors" to "We could make our own clothes, but you'd have to buy us a sewing machine." In the end the idea that appealed to them most came from Jessica, my twelve-year-old. "Give each of us the money and we'll manage it ourselves." She even volunteered to help her sisters with their budgets.

I agreed, even though I had my doubts. I'm not sure the younger ones fully understand all the implications of their solution, but it has already had an effect upon Jessica. I was helping her shop for a sweater and pointed to a pretty blue one on the rack. She went right for the price tag and said, "Mom, I don't believe you. This is much too expensive!"

*　　*　　*

THIS NEXT STORY WAS FROM A MOTHER WHO WAS COPING WITH her three-year-old's separation anxiety.

All the other mothers dropped their children off at preschool with a cheerful good-bye, but Allison would get hysterical whenever I started to move toward the door. She'd run after me and hang on to my arm and cry bitterly. I was starting to feel desperate. It was three weeks into the term and she showed no sign of letting up.

One morning I decided to try problem solving. After breakfast I sat her on my lap and said, "Allison, you really like me to stay with you at preschool, and (notice I said 'and,' not 'but') today I need to leave to do my errands. So I was wondering what we could do?"

She looked at me blankly. I said, "Would it help if you had your teddy bear with you?" She shook her head no. "How about my fuzzy scarf?" She shook her head again and buried her face in my shoulder. "You stay," she said. And then a minute later, "Go. But give me eleventy hugs."

Suddenly I had an inspiration. I took her hand, kissed her palm, and closed it. I said, "Now you have my kiss. Quick, put it in your pocket and whenever you miss me, you can take it out and give yourself a kiss from Mommy. What do you think of that?"

Her face lit up. She shoved her "kiss" deep in her pocket and that morning, for the first time, she let me go.

*   *   *

THIS NEXT CONVERSATION WAS REPORTED BY THE FATHER OF A fourteen-year-old boy who was being pressured by his peers to drink.

My son, Zack, knows how I feel about drugs and alcohol. I've always tried to give him straight information—no scare tactics. Recently I heard rumors that the kids were going to this one particular house after school when the parents weren't home and drinking. When I drove Zack to basketball practice, I told him what I'd heard and asked him if it was true. He looked at me uneasily but didn't answer.

"Did you ever drink?" I asked.

"I had a beer once," he said.

Before I could say anything, he burst out, "Dad, I had to! Everyone makes fun of you if you don't."

I wanted to say, "So if everyone makes fun of you for not jumping off the Brooklyn Bridge, do you jump?" Instead I said, "So you're under a lot of pressure from your peers."

"You'd better believe it!" he said. "You should hear what they call the kids who don't drink."

I told him I could see what he was up against, but I also said, "You know how I feel about drugs, and alcohol is a drug. Even if it were legal to drink at your age, I'd object. You've told me that you don't like me to 'control you.' But what I've observed about kids and grown-ups who drink is that sometimes the drink ends up controlling them."

"So what do you want me to do?" Zack said belligerently. "Say something dumb like 'I don't need it; I'm high on life'? "

I said, "Is that the problem? How to say no and remain part of the crowd?"

Zack shrugged, but I knew that was it. For the rest of the ride we played around with lines he could use to refuse a drink diplomatically. The one Zack thought least "nerdy" was "Thanks, maybe later." And if pressed, to blame it on his strict parents: "You don't know my father. He'd kill me if he smelled liquor on my breath. I'd be grounded for the rest of my life!"

Zack chuckled over that one and gave me a big "Thanks, Dad" when I dropped him off at his game.

Questions from Teachers

1. Do you have to go through all the steps of the problem solving process for it to work?

Not necessarily. One teacher described how nine-year-old Spencer, a serious, hardworking student, became angry whenever the other children in his science group fooled around or stopped working—even for a few minutes. One day he lost all control and threw books and papers on the floor. The teacher decided that this latest development warranted the full problem-solving approach.

She sat down with him and started with "Spencer, I can see how much it upsets you when the other children in your group begin to joke around. Once you start on a project, you don't like to have any interruptions."

Almost immediately Spencer responded, "Yeah, because I want to finish and they make me forget what I'm doing." Then, after a short pause, he stood up and said, "Can I go to the back table and work alone when they start to mess around?"

The teacher was startled. She said, "You think that would help?" He nodded and said, "That way I won't get so mad and throw things." And from that moment on, that's how Spencer coped.

2. One of my students, Debby, can never remember to bring her books to school. I tried to problem solve with her, but got nowhere. She just joked around and acted silly. Any suggestions?

If a child resists your efforts to problem solve, a note based upon the same principles can serve as an effective substitute. For example, you might write:

Dear Debby,

You told me that it's hard for you to remember to bring your books to school and that sometimes you "just forget."

I need to know that all of my students have their books with them *every day* so that they can do their work.

Please think of a way to remind yourself to bring your books with you each morning. I'll think, too. Then let's exchange ideas and see which one you want to put into action.

Sincerely,
Mrs. G.

3. When a teacher and student are thinking about possible solutions together, is it really necessary to write them down? Isn't it enough to simply tell them to each other?

Sometimes it is. However, don't underestimate the rush of pride and pleasure that wells up within a child at seeing his ideas taken seriously enough to be written down by his teacher. The sight of his words on paper not only gives him a visual appreciation of his thought process but inspires him to continue to think creatively.

4. Last week I was problem solving with a girl in my class about her chronic lateness. We were making steady progress until we got to the part where we were supposed to start brainstorming together. I immediately offered two excellent suggestions. She immediately clammed up. What went wrong?

It's always a good idea to wait after asking a child to brainstorm with you. Let *her* come up with the first few ideas. Your silence is an invitation, a mark of respect, a way of saying that thoughts need time to form and grow. When an adult moves in too quickly—even with the most "excellent" of suggestions—the child often feels less able to generate an excellent suggestion of her own.

5. I'm worried about the increasing incidence of violence in my school—sometimes over an issue as trivial as a dirty look. Since problem-solving skills seem to be so effective when we use them with students, why couldn't children be taught these skills so they could use them with each other?

You'll be glad to know that in programs across the country students from kindergarten age on up through high school are receiving training in conflict resolution skills.[1] A growing number of educators are convinced that since conflict between human beings is inevitable, learning how to deal with disagreements and resolve them peacefully is as important a subject for children as math or social studies. In schools where these programs are in effect, teachers report:

> What I like about the program is that the kids are putting out their own fires. And that frees me to teach.
>
> I love seeing these fourth and fifth graders out there with their clipboards and orange "Conflict Manager" T-shirts. Ever since we instituted the training, the lunchroom, playground, and classrooms have become much more peaceful places.
>
> It amazes me to see how after a fifteen-hour course, some of the worst kids in the school become

[1]The Community Board Program in San Francisco; Project SMART (School Mediators' Alternative Resolution Team) in New York City; Hawaii School Mediation Alliance in Kahili.

the best mediators. I think they do better than we do with the kids who "act out," because they speak the same language.

Everyone seems to agree that young people who have mastered the skills for listening to each other with respect and seeing a conflict as a problem to be solved rather than a battle to be won are our best hope for a peaceful world.

Stories from Teachers

THIS FIRST STORY ILLUSTRATES HOW THE PROBLEM-SOLVING approach helped a teacher get to the root of a problem.

Jenny is a delightful twelve-year-old except when we're doing math. Then she turns into a demanding, whiny baby who can't work on her own. Talk about math anxiety!

Over the school year I tried every strategy I knew to give her confidence. I even had her tested so she could get extra help if she needed it, but her scores were too high to qualify her for the resource room. I finally ended up ignoring her. Result? She stopped working altogether. In sheer desperation I decided to go the problem-solving route. Here's what happened:

Me:	Jenny, I know how much you worry about doing math.
Jenny:	I do. I just hate the stuff.
Me:	Because some of it seems too hard?
Jenny:	Yes . . . And I make mistakes.

Me:	And that upsets you.
Jenny:	Yeah, because then you'll be mad at me. Last year Mr. G. yelled at me for being stupid and making so many mistakes.

I was stunned.

Me:	Is that what has you worried? You think I'll yell, too?
Jenny:	(teary-eyed) Uh-huh.
Me :	(taking her hands in mine) Jenny, you've got to give yourself permission to make lots of mistakes. That's something all good students know. Mistakes can be useful. Annoying, but useful.
Jenny:	Useful?
Me:	Yes, because they tell you what you still need to learn. Besides, sometimes a mistake can lead to a discovery. Look what Columbus found from his mistake.
Jenny:	(big smile) America! . . . So you won't be mad if I get the wrong answer?
Me:	No, Jenny. I just wish there were a way you could do your math without worrying so much about getting it "right."
Jenny:	Maybe I could try to get the answer by myself . . . but if I can't . . . ?
Me:	I'll help you. And if I'm busy, maybe your friend Claudia can help you.

Over the next few weeks I could see Jenny working longer and harder on her own. She asked if she could sit next to Claudia, but they didn't compare answers until Jenny was finished with her work. I think what helped her turn a corner was not so much being near her friend as knowing that making a mistake was not a catastrophe.

* * *

THIS LAST EXAMPLE CAME FROM A SPECIAL EDUCATION TEACHER who taught in an inner city school.[2] She said, "Many of my kids are products of physical and emotional abuse. They come to school like firecrackers ready to explode. I can't get through a period without a fight erupting. One will say, 'You're stupid,' or 'Your mother,' or kick someone under the table and there goes my lesson."

Despite her doubts, she decided to try problem solving to see what might come of it. Here are excerpts from her written report.

I decided that if the first step of problem solving was to find out how the kids really felt about fighting, I should start by asking them what was good about fighting. Here's the list we developed:

WHAT'S GOOD ABOUT FIGHTING

1. Getting back!! (This was definitely the most popular)
2. Getting someone in trouble
3. Getting someone to chase you
4. Snapping (insulting) is funny
5. They won't mess with you again
6. You feel like it

[2]Reprinted with permission from an article by Adele Faber and Elaine Mazlish in the Summer 1987 issue of the *American Educator*, the quarterly journal of the American Federation of Teachers.

7. They start up first
8. Class is boring (Teacher's contribution)
9. Getting someone mad
10. It's fun to play rough

They were pretty rambunctious as we were working out the list. Then I asked, "What's bad about fighting?" and they became solemn. Here's what they said:

WHAT'S BAD ABOUT FIGHTING

1. After you fight, you feel bad if it's your friend
2. You can get into trouble—with mother, teacher, principal
3. It puts your teacher in a bad mood (Teacher's contribution)
4. You can hurt somebody
5. You can get suspended
6. You don't get to learn (Teacher's contribution)
7. It could start a worse fight
8. You could get hurt—beaten up, scratched, bitten, black eye

Then we went to work on trying to think of solutions. I thought twice about writing down some of their suggestions, but then I remembered that it was important not to reject any of their ideas.

POSSIBLE SOLUTIONS

1. Ask to go out and let off steam
2. Hit him
3. Walk away
4. Pound the clay
5. Squeeze hand grippers

6. Break a stick
7. Call his mother
8. Let them fight it out in the gym with no crowd
9. Tell the teacher
10. Change your seat
11. Tell him to leave you alone
12. Send him to the office
13. Make him write something 100 times
14. Make him lick the floor
15. Everybody hit him once
16. Give stickers to the ones who follow the rules
17. Write something mean to him
18. Say something nice back to him to make him embarrassed

After we had all 18 items listed, I commented on some of them. For example, I told them I couldn't allow them to fight it out, because I didn't want them hurting each other. Also, licking the floor didn't seem very sanitary to me. They all had strong opinions about the rest of the list, each preferring different solutions. After more discussion and more suggestions, we agreed that each student should copy into his notebook the solutions that made the most sense to him.

At the end of the period, we wrote on the board the rules we could all agree to:

1. **NO INSULTS**
2. **NO CURSES**
3. **DON'T TELL ON ANYONE ELSE UNLESS THEY ARE BOTHERING YOU**
4. **NO HITTING OR THROWING**
5. **USE YOUR OWN SOLUTIONS!!!**

Here are the results of that day:

- Luis, who has the shortest fuse, walks out of the room several times a week. He stands in the doorway so he won't miss anything. After a while, he comes in and sits at the back of the room. After a few minutes more, he joins the class.
- Every once in a while, one student will pop up and say, "Carlos, change with me!" and change his seat. (Carlos is pretty good-natured about changing.)
- Twice a student pounded the clay.
- Once Darren said, "Give him the clay to pound!"
- When one student insults another, the class calls out, "Rule number one!" or, "Rule number two!" They also say, "Make him read the rule!" and the "offender" will read the rule.
- They also decided that they would not even insult the garbage can. (Once Darren said, "Your mother," to the garbage can and Luis thought Darren was saying it to him, and it started a fight, so the class added a new rule about not cursing "things.")

I wish I could say that putting this whole approach into action came naturally to me. It didn't. It took thought, effort, and a lot more time than I wanted to spend. It would have been much easier for me to write these kids off as "incorrigible" or "hopeless." Yet by treating them as "problem solvers," that's what they became.

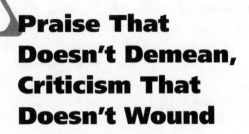

Praise That Doesn't Demean, Criticism That Doesn't Wound

"PLEASE . . . HAVE A SEAT. WE HAVE A LOT
TO DISCUSS."

I shifted nervously in the seat across from the principal's desk.

"Ms. Lander, as I'm sure you know, for the first three years of teaching you are on probation." (My mind started to race. "'Probation'—isn't that for convicted criminals?")

"Every year for three years you will have a minimum of three evaluations. This is your first. I want you to know that I believe you have a lot of potential . . . *but* you are going to have to work to earn tenure. Now is the time to learn from your mistakes. Let's look at Monday's lesson to see what went wrong."

Reaching into a file cabinet, he pulled out a manila folder stamped PROBATIONARY in red block letters. Then he leaned back in his chair and, with his glasses poised on the bridge of his nose, leafed through the copious notes he'd made during his observation of my lesson. "Let's see . . . I believe the purpose of your lesson was to teach the students how to write a letter. Am I correct?"

"Yes, Mr. Steele." (What was he getting at?)

"You told the students that you had a book with celebrities' names and addresses in it so that they could write to the star of their choice. *That was your first mistake.* As soon as you told them about the possibility of contacting a celebrity, they stopped listening to you and began talking to each other. You lost them. Instead of focusing on the protocol for letter writing, they were discussing celebrities. In the future I suggest that you refer to the district guidelines for curricular decisions. If you follow these guidelines with your students, they will be better prepared to take the state writing assessment in the spring. While employed in this district, you need to teach the standards as written."

I tried to defend myself. "I thought that if I generated a little enthusiasm for the letter writing . . ."

"That brings us to my next point. The students' enthusiasm was expressed in a number of inappropriate ways. During your half-hour lesson three notes were passed, mouth noises were made, a desk was pounded on, and one student got out of his seat to talk to a classmate. Were you aware that all of that activity was going on in the back of the class?"

"Well, yes . . . but the kids were just a little excited, Mr. Steele."

He leaned forward in his chair. "Ms. Lander, we have specific standards for conduct in our classrooms. You may not be aware of how quickly a problem can escalate. Students of this age are very volatile. If they aren't kept in line, the situation can easily get out of control. Even if we work with this celebrity letter idea, improvements can be made. I suggest you keep the focus of your lesson on the correct form of writing a letter and spend less time discussing which celebrities your students admire."

The secretary's voice came over the intercom. "Mr. Steele, the superintendent is on line one. Would you like to take the call or shall I take a message?"

Mr. Steele looked at his watch. "I'd better take it," he said as he flipped through more of his notes. "Well . . . I have several other points to discuss with you, but perhaps you have enough to work on for now. I suggest you sit in on Mrs. Harding's class. She's a fine teacher. You could hear a pin drop in her room. Let's schedule a second meeting for tomorrow, so we can finish smoothing out the rough spots."

Back in my empty classroom, I closed the door behind me and mindlessly sifted through the pile of papers on my desk. Tears welled up in my eyes. Didn't he like anything about my lesson? Sure the kids were a little rowdy, but I'd rather have them excited about the topic than slumped in their seats looking comatose. I wanted them to care about what they wrote, whether it was to a celebrity or a friend or someone in Congress. Isn't what they write just as important as *how* they write? I looked again at the stack of uncorrected letters lying on my desk, picked up my red pencil, and put it down again. I had no desire to mark those papers. No desire to teach. No desire ever to set foot in a classroom again.

I heard a knock at the door. It was Maria carrying a folder filled with student drawings. "Sorry to bother you," she said cheerfully, "but could I borrow your stapler?"

"Sure."

"You okay?" Maria asked, staring at me.

"I just had a rough afternoon. I don't know . . . I'm beginning to think I should have gone into business instead of teaching."

"How can you say such a thing? You're a wonderful teacher. One of the best! I think you're outstanding!"

I looked up at Maria. She was smiling down at me, searching my face for a return smile. I managed to mumble, "Thank you, Maria," and handed her the stapler.

A moment after she left, Jane entered. "You look as if someone kicked you in the stomach," she observed.

I told myself to be "professional" and not burden Jane with my troubles. But one look at her face, and I blurted out the whole story.

Jane listened and shook her head sympathetically.

"And to top it off," I said tearfully, "he said I was too animated, that I couldn't control my class, and that I should sit in on Mrs. Harding's class to see how a *good* teacher teaches."

"Mrs. Harding?" Jane sneered.

"He said you can hear a pin drop in her room."

"That's because the kids are asleep."

"Jane," I burst out, "don't joke. He took the heart out of me."

"I know . . . I know. I'm just mad that you had to be subjected to Steele's warped idea of 'constructive criticism.' "

"Maria was just in." I sniffled. "She's such a dear. She tried to make me feel better. Told me I was a wonderful teacher."

"But you didn't believe her."

"I wanted to. But all I could think about when she said that were all the times I wasn't so wonderful."

"That's the way it seems to go," Jane sighed. "Criticism can knock the stuffings out of you. And praise like 'You're great . . . wonderful . . . marvelous' is too much for anyone to take."

"I know. I wanted to tell Maria she was all wrong about me."

"Because it's hard to accept such extravagant praise. Did you ever notice how uncomfortable you get whenever anyone evaluates you? I know the minute someone tells me I'm 'good' or 'pretty' or 'smart,' all I can think about are the times I was bad or felt ugly or did something dumb."

"That's just what happened! As Maria was insisting that I was 'the best,' I thought of last Monday when I came to school tired, poorly prepared, and terrified that the principal would pay me a surprise visit."

Jane laughed out loud. "She meant well. People always mean well when they praise you. They just don't know how."

"What is there to know?"

"That instead of *evaluating* what someone has done, you need to *describe* it."

"*Describe it?*"

"Right. You need to describe—in detail—exactly what it is the person did."

"I don't get it. Give me an example."

Jane looked at me intently. "Okay," she said. "Liz, you were required to teach your class how to write a formal letter and you could easily have settled for a standard lesson. But you knew that kids don't usually get turned on by headings and salutations and inside addresses. So you gave the subject some thought and came up with a motivation that fired your students' imaginations and had them writing with passion and purpose *and* correct form."

I sat up in my seat. "That *is* what I did!" I exclaimed. "It could easily have been a boring lesson, but I *did* get the kids excited and involved. And they *did* learn how to write a formal letter. . . . You know what? I don't care what anyone says. It was a very good lesson."

"Aha!" said Jane triumphantly. "Look what just happened! All I did was describe what you did, and you, recognizing the truth of my words, credited yourself."

Maria returned with the stapler and apologized for interrupting us.

"Maria," I said, "don't go. You've got to hear what Jane has been telling me about praise. I want to know what you think of it. Jane, please say it all over again."

Jane obliged. She told Maria that children have trouble accepting praise that evaluates them. She said, "Telling a child 'You're so well organized' usually leads to 'Not really.' But the kind of praise that a child can 'take in' and that truly builds self-esteem comes in two parts. First, *the adult describes what the child has done.* ('I see you're all ready for school tomorrow. You finished your homework, sharpened your pencils, packed your books, and even made your lunch.') Second, *the child, after hearing his accomplishment described, praises himself.* ('I know to organize and plan ahead.')"

Maria looked distressed. "I don't understand," she said. "All I know is that the way I was raised wasn't good. My mother and father believed that they shouldn't say nice things about the children to their faces because they could get big heads. But I think children should get compliments. It helps them to be proud of themselves. I always tell Marco and Ana Ruth how good they are and how smart they are."

Very gently Jane said, "So you wanted your children to have what you never did."

Maria closed her eyes and nodded. "But maybe I overdo it. When I tell Marco how smart he is, he says, 'Raphael is smarter.' When I tell Ana Ruth what a great violinist she is, she says, 'Mama, stop bragging about me.'"

"That's the point I've been trying to make," Jane said. "Children become very uncomfortable with praise that evaluates them. They push it away. Sometimes they'll deliberately misbehave to prove you wrong."

Maria stared at her. "Oh, my goodness," she said. "Now I understand what happened in Mr. Peterson's class when I was helping out yesterday."

"What do you mean?" I asked.

"This boy, Brian, who drives everybody crazy, finally sat in his seat and finished his work. So I patted him on his back and told him he was a good boy. I thought that would encourage him to keep on behaving himself, but it didn't. He crossed his eyes and let his tongue hang out of the side of his mouth and he fell out of his seat. I couldn't understand it."

I was confused. "And now you do?" I asked.

"Well, according to what Jane has been saying, he *had* to make nothing of my compliment. It made him too nervous. He couldn't live up to it. He had to show me that he wasn't really good."

"But he was good," I protested. "For the moment."

"Then Maria could have described the moment," Jane said.

"Yes," Maria agreed. "Maybe I should have told him . . ."

That was the beginning of what turned out to be a long, animated discussion among the three of us. Describing a child's accomplishments, rather than evaluating them with an easy "good" or "great," turned out to be harder than we thought—not because it was difficult to describe, but because we were so unaccustomed to doing it. However, once we got into the swing of looking carefully at a child's achievement and putting into words what we saw or felt, we did it more and more easily and with ever-growing pleasure. On the next two pages you'll see, in cartoon form, some of the examples we worked out showing how parents and teachers can use descriptive praise.

DESCRIPTIVE PRAISE AT HOME

DESCRIPTIVE PRAISE IN THE CLASSROOM

As we studied the examples we had worked out, we had many additional thoughts to share with each other.

Me: Descriptive praise takes work, doesn't it? If you're going to tell a child what you see or feel, then you have to really look and pay attention. It's much easier to say "That's great" or "Fantastic" or "Terrific." You don't even need to think for that kind of praise.

Jane: It's true. Descriptive praise is harder and takes longer, but look at the payoff for the child.

Maria: I understand what you're saying, but if a child has always been criticized and has never heard any praise at all, wouldn't it be better for him to hear "You're a good boy" instead of nothing?

Jane: If a kid is starving, even cotton candy is better than nothing. But why settle for so little? We want to give our children the kind of emotional nourishment that will help them become independent, creative thinkers and doers. If we train them to constantly look to others for approval, what message are we sending them?

Me: You can't trust yourself. You need everybody else's opinion to tell you how you're doing.

Maria: That's not a good message, is it?

Jane: No, because we want our children to trust their own judgment, to have enough confidence to be able to say to themselves "I'm satisfied" or "I'm not satisfied with what I've done." And to make corrections or adjustments based upon their *own* evaluations.

That evening I found myself actually looking forward to reading and correcting the letters my students had written. The first one was a pleasant surprise. Instead of *"Very good!"* I wrote: *"A pleasure to read. Clear topic sentences and lively examples of how Michael Jordan affected your life."* The second paper didn't disappoint either. I wrote: *"A thoughtful exploration of the problems of homeless people. My guess is the president will find your original proposal very interesting."*

I swelled with pride at the high level of my students' writing and took full credit for having inspired it. (So much for you, Mr. Steele.) The next paper looked as if it were written by a second grader. It was Melissa's letter to Barbra Streisand and it barely filled half a page. I picked up my red pencil and wrote: *"Poor work. No inside address. Where's the date? Misspelled words. Undeveloped content."*

I looked again at my big, red, angry comments and thought, "How could I do that to Melissa?" That's the kind of criticism Mr. Steele threw at me. . . . I was stopped in my tracks. It wasn't hard to praise what you liked, but how do you criticize what you don't like? How do you point out what's wrong without demoralizing the person you're criticizing? Was there any way that Mr. Steele could have expressed his displeasure to me without discouraging me completely?

I stared out the window. Maybe if he had started by appreciating what I *had* accomplished—however little—I could have heard what bothered him without going to pieces. Maybe if he had said something like "Liz, you've achieved your goals. You motivated your students to learn how to write a letter. The one thing I see that still remains to be worked on is how to generate enthusiasm for your topic and still maintain order." If he had said that, I could have heard him. More than that. I would have given serious thought as to how to prevent the kids' excitement from getting out of hand in the future.

Maybe that was the key to helping children improve. *Instead of focusing on what's wrong, start by acknowledging what a child* has *accomplished. Then point out what still needs to be done.*

Okay, now what could I write on Melissa's paper? She hadn't accomplished anything. Or had she? I looked again and found it.

I took out my eraser and made a red blur on Melissa's paper. Then I carefully inked in my new comments. I wrote: *"I like your line, 'You are my favorite of favorites.' I think Ms. Streisand will like it, too. I also think she would enjoy seeing an example of exactly what it is you admire about her. Please check your paper to make sure all underlined words are spelled correctly and that you've included the date and inside address. I look forward to reading your revised letter."*

It seemed to me that I'd come upon an important principle. Yes, we can all, teachers and students and parents, benefit from having an outsider with an objective point of view tell us how we can do better. But before we can even consider making changes, we need to believe that there is more right with us than wrong and that we have the power to fix whatever is wrong. To help myself imagine how this theory would work in other situations, I thought of two examples that might occur—one in the home setting and one at school:

AN ALTERNATIVE TO CRITICISM

AT HOME

INSTEAD OF POINTING OUT WHAT'S WRONG . . .

DESCRIBE WHAT'S RIGHT AND WHAT STILL NEEDS TO BE DONE.

IN SCHOOL

INSTEAD OF POINTING OUT WHAT HASN'T BEEN DONE . . .

DESCRIBE WHAT HAS BEEN DONE AND WHAT NEEDS TO BE DONE.

Over the next few weeks I found myself thinking a great deal about praise and criticism. Mr. Steele's "constructive criticism" had left me hurting and discouraged. Maria's extravagant praise had left me feeling unconvinced and unworthy. But Jane's straightforward description of what I had tried to accomplish had put me together, restored my faith in myself, and given me the impetus to do even better next time.

What a simple yet amazing process! I suppose that what Jane did for me is what we all ought to do for one another as we work at meeting the challenges of our lives.

- Teachers need to be affirmed as they struggle to meet the needs of all their students.
- Parents need to be affirmed as they contend with the daily difficulties of raising their children.
- Children need to be affirmed as they try to understand their world and find their place in it.

In my perfect universe we would all be there for one another, holding up a mirror to one another's efforts and accomplishments so that we could all feel visible and valued.

HELPFUL PRAISE
At Home and in School

Child: Listen to my poem about a train. Tell me if it's good.

Adult: Beautiful! You're a great poet.

Instead of evaluating:

1. DESCRIBE WHAT YOU SEE OR HEAR.

"You caught the 'chug-a-chug' rhythm of a train and you found a way to rhyme 'track' with 'clickity clack.'"

2. DESCRIBE WHAT YOU FEEL.

"It makes me feel as if I'm sitting inside a railroad car speeding through the countryside."

Adult: Look at those misspelled words—you can do better than that.

Instead of criticizing:

3. POINT OUT WHAT NEEDS TO BE DONE.

"All this poem needs now is the correct spelling of the words 'caboose' and 'freight' and it's ready for the bulletin board."

Questions and Stories from Parents and Teachers

Questions from Parents

1. My son is a terrific kid and I am always complimenting him. But yesterday he said to me, "Mom, you notice me too much." Is there such a thing as too much praise?

Your son's reaction is not unusual. Most children become very uneasy at hearing a running commentary about their behavior—even if all the comments are positive. They feel as if they're under constant surveillance. Other children have a very different reaction to "being noticed" all the time. They become so accustomed to hearing an appreciative comment about everything they do that they feel lost without it and become less confident about themselves.

Still other children experience constant praise as a subtle, unspoken directive to get them to perform according to their parents' standards and wishes. Often these children conclude, "I have to give up thinking about what *I* want to do and how *I* want to do it and think about what *they* want me to do. I can't trust me. I'd better trust them."

2. My daughter was in the middle of making a diorama of an Early American kitchen and asked me what I thought of it. I told her I thought her teacher would probably give it an A. Was that okay?

Whenever there's a choice between directing your child's attention to the approval of others or turning her back to her task, choose the task. You can tell your daughter, "You took an old cardboard box and you're slowly transforming it into a Colonial kitchen. I see a spinning wheel and a fireplace and . . . how did you get the little cradle to look so real?" The most valuable kind of learning takes place when children are deeply involved in what they're doing, not when they're worried about how others will judge them.

3. My son finally brought home a report card with straight A's. I told him how proud I was of him. Is that okay?

Any time you're uncertain as to whether your praise is helpful or not, you can ask yourself a key question: "Are my words making my child more dependent upon me and my approval, or do my words help him to see his strengths and give him a clearer picture of *his abilities* and *his accomplishments?*" Contrast the following statements:

PRAISE THAT CREATES DEPENDENCY UPON THE APPROVAL OF OTHERS	PRAISE THAT GIVES A CHILD A SENSE OF HIS OWN ABILITIES AND ACCOMPLISHMENTS
• "A perfect report card. I'm so proud of you."	• "These A's represent determination and hours of hard work. You must be proud of yourself."
• "Doing your homework? Good girl!"	• "It takes self-discipline to do your homework when you're feeling tired."
• "You're a very generous person."	• "When you saw that Elliot forgot his sandwich, you gave him part of yours."

181

Notice how the comments in the first column put the *parents* in control. They're the ones who have the power to bestow the praise or withhold it. The statements in the second column put *the child* in touch with his own powers and enable him to praise himself.

4. Can't you ever tell a child directly that he's "considerate" or "honest" or "creative"?

Any kind of approval can feel good for the moment. But if you want these words to go inside a child and remain there, you need to follow or precede them with a description. For example:

> You knew I'd be worried if you weren't home when I got back from work, so you left me a note with a phone number where I could reach you. That's what I call being *considerate*.

> You told me what happened in school today even though you knew that I might get angry. I appreciate your *honesty*.

> What a *creative* collage! It has string and pasta and buttons and fringes made of toilet paper.

In each case you are pointing out a single instance in which a child has been considerate or honest or creative. There is no pressure for him to always be that way.

5. I have two daughters. The younger is an honor student, but the older one struggles to get B's and C's. When they both show me their report cards at the same time, I try to avoid praising the younger one so that her older sister won't feel bad. Am I doing the right thing?

182

Your response to one child's accomplishments should have nothing to do with what her sister has or hasn't accomplished. Each child needs to be affirmed for her individual achievements. Your younger daughter is entitled to time alone with you so that she can share her pride in her academic ability and have it acknowledged by her mother. Her older sister is also entitled to private "report card time" so that she can express her satisfaction or dissatisfaction with her schoolwork and receive support for her efforts. Neither of your daughters should receive less than her due because of her sister's talents.

Stories from Parents

THIS EXPERIENCE WAS REPORTED BY A MOTHER WHO DISCOVERED for herself how evaluative praise inhibited her child's creative process and how descriptive praise released it.

When my daughter, Jami, was in kindergarten, she had a chance to enter an art contest. She didn't seem interested, but I pushed her into it. I suppose it's because I'm an artist. While she was drawing, I sat down beside her and kept saying, "That's great! . . . Wow, I like that color. . . . How about the feet? . . . Shouldn't they be a little bigger? . . . That's it! Stop! That is *perfect!*"

After a few seconds Jami said, "Mom, why must it be perfect?" Then she put down her crayon and refused to do any more. At first I was upset with her. Then I realized that I probably talked too much. So the next time she brought a drawing home from school, I made no comment. But I guess she wanted me to say something, because she stuck it in front of my face while I was folding the laundry. It was a picture of a tiger and it was really good. With a few minor changes it could've been fantastic. But I controlled myself. I picked it up and just described: "I see you made a smiling tiger with orange and black stripes and a long tail and . . ." Before I could go on, Jami pulled it away from me and said, "This is the mommy. Now I'm going to make the baby tiger."

Afterward, when I thought about what happened, I realized that all my "helpful" comments were my way of getting her to please me, when the person she really needed to please was herself. From now on I'm going to try and keep out of her way when she's drawing. I guess the only time she needs a comment from me is when she asks for it.

* * *

THIS WAS FROM ANOTHER MOTHER WHO DISCOVERED WHAT CAN happen when you resist the urge to evaluate.

I returned home from a workshop on descriptive praise and noticed a picture lying on the kitchen counter drawn by my twelve-year-old son, John. It was evident that he had left it there for me to see. As I walked past his room, he sat up in bed and asked, "Did you see my picture?"

Usually my response would've been "Yes, it's beautiful. You're really a wonderful artist." But being fresh from my workshop, I thought, "Okay, I'll try to describe." So I said, "Why, yes. I saw a huge Plateosaurus floating in a lake and big trees and boulders on the shore and a highway stretching across the land."

John smiled from ear to ear and began to share with me what he had learned about "Champ," a sea monster spotted in Lake Champlain. As he went on about what excited him, I felt we were really connecting with each other. It was the kind of moment I treasure. And to think that it doesn't have to happen willy-nilly, but that I can make it happen, really excites me.

*   *   *

THIS NEXT STORY FROM A WORKING MOTHER DESCRIBES A SITUATION that could easily have caused her to scold her children. Instead she turned it into an opportunity to praise them.

Ever since I took a part-time job, I've had many crises with my being late and my three children being locked out of the house after school. Finally, I decided to hide a spare key outside the house and told the kids to use it only in an emergency and to be sure to return it to its hiding place as soon as the door was opened.

That turned out to be a great solution because at least once a week I had to work overtime. Then one afternoon I came back to the house late and found my three kids sitting around the table having an after-school snack and there, on the kitchen floor, was the key.

I said, "Oh, no, how did our key get on the floor?"

My son, Nicky, said, "Oh, I forgot to put it back."

I could see that he felt terrible about it, so I told

him that I thought that it was pretty good.

The kids all looked at me in surprise. I said, "Do you realize how responsible you three have been about the key? You've been using it for over a year now and this is the first and only time someone has forgotten to return it. I think that's a record to be proud of."

The three of them beamed. Then Nicky jumped up from the table and said, "I'll put it back now."

I never had to remind them again.

* * *

IN THIS ACCOUNT YOU CAN SEE HOW A SON PRESENTED HIS "worst" to his mother and how she found a way to help him see his "best."

Paul wasn't a great student. He believed in doing the least he could in the shortest amount of time in order to "get by." One afternoon after school he came into the house and just stood there. I took one look at his face and became alarmed. "What happened?" I asked.

He said, "I just kicked in the garage door."

I was shocked. "On purpose?"

"I failed my algebra test!" he blurted out. "And I tried! I really tried this time. I studied. And I failed."

He was clearly in so much pain that I told myself that this was not the time to focus on the garage door. I felt terrible for him. For years now his father and I had been after him to apply himself, to try harder, and here he had finally done it. He'd honestly tried to do his best and it turned out that his best had resulted in failure.

"Well, aren't you going to ground me?" he demanded.

I didn't know how to respond. I only knew I had better hang on to whatever skills I had to keep us both from drowning. Tentatively I asked, "Did you bring the test home?"

He reached into his backpack and threw the paper on my bed. It had a sixty scrawled across the top. I studied the paper and tried to figure out what went wrong. I said, "Paul, please, I can see how upset you are, but I need you to explain this to me. This first example, the one you got right, how did you arrive at the answer?"

Paul explained a long, complex process to me—something about factoring a polynomial into a binomial. I tried to follow him, but couldn't. When he was finished, I said, "So you understood the theory, even though I don't, and you must have understood these other five examples because you got them right, too. What went wrong with the other four?"

Paul leaned over the paper and said, "In these two I multiplied where I should have divided and in these two I just made stupid mistakes in addition."

"So what you're telling me," I said slowly, "is that you understand all this complicated stuff, but that you made four careless errors that cost you forty points. All I can conclude is that you have a mind that can grasp advanced mathematical concepts, but that you need to make yourself check your calculations before you hand in your paper."

Almost before my very eyes the tension drained from Paul's face. As he left the room, I took my first deep breath and felt as if I had passed some kind of test myself.

Ten minutes later Paul returned. He said, "Don't worry about the garage door, Mom. I used the hammer, very gently, and I was able to straighten it out." "Thanks," I said.

Questions from Teachers

1. I have a girl in my class named Jessica who is outstanding. I'm torn between my urge to praise her enthusiastically all the time and my worry that the other kids will begin to resent her and see her as the teacher's pet. Any suggestions?

Trust your worry. You do Jessica no favor by constantly making public comments about how "outstanding" she is. It would be better for her and everyone else if you were to look for opportunities to show your appreciation for the entire class: "What teamwork! You all pitched in and did such a thorough cleanup, the custodian won't even suspect we did a science project today."

When you're especially pleased by something Jessica has done, you can describe it matter-of-factly: "I see how you managed to add up this long column of figures and get the right answer. It's because you were careful to put one number directly under the other." That's the kind of objective comment the other students can hear comfortably and possibly profit from. It would be best to save your emotional response to Jessica for a more private moment. That's when you can tell her why and how much you enjoy having her in your class.

2. Are there any objections to pointing out to a student that she's the best writer in the class or that he scored the highest mark on the math final?

The problem with focusing on who is the "best" or "fastest" or "brightest" is twofold: The rest of the class can easily become discouraged. Some might stop trying altogether. And the star must now use all his energies not on his personal goals but on maintaining his stardom. Now his continued success rests upon the continued failure of his classmates. It would be much more helpful for your student to hear his accomplishments described without any reference to his peers. For example: "You portrayed your grandparents' farm in such detail that I could almost see it." Or, "Every answer on this paper is correct. You really understand decimal points." Statements like these help a student to measure himself by his own standards rather than against his classmates' performance.

3. In my last school there was a heavy emphasis on having the children recite, "I am special." . . . "I am lovable." . . . "I am capable." The teachers were also encouraged to give out gold stars and stickers with smiley faces. Do you consider the above methods effective ways to build self-esteem?

You can't paste self-esteem on from the outside. The affirmations and stickers you describe may adhere momentarily, but they fall off easily when the evidence suggests to the child that he *isn't* so lovable or capable or special. On the other hand, words that describe what the child is doing, or has done, last forever and can be called on in time of need. For example, if a student is worried about writing a report on whales, telling himself "I am special" or looking at his collection of gold stars will do him little good. But if his recent report on redwood trees had a comment like "Full of interesting information. I learned things about these living giants that I had never known before," then the student might say to himself, "I did it before. I guess I can do it again."

4. You suggest that a teacher be quick to acknowledge whatever effort a student makes. But suppose a child asks a question that shows total ignorance. At one point don't you have to tell her she's wrong and give her the right answer?

Our role as educators is not to supply "right" answers *but to help children arrive at answers through their own thinking process.* You can start by respectfully asking a student what thoughts prompted her question and lead her to the next level of understanding with additional questions.

A special education teacher reported that she was reading a story to her class about a beekeeper when Charlene raised her hand and asked, "Do a bee be a bird?" The class was electrified by the question. Several children raised their hands and waved them eagerly.

The teacher said, "Wait a minute. Charlene, that's such an interesting question! What makes you think that a bee could be a bird?"

Very solemnly Charlene replied, "They both got wings."

"Is there anything else that's the same?"

"They fly."

"You noticed two things that were the same. Class, is there anything that makes birds different from bees?"

"Birds got feathers."

"Birds is bigger."

"Birds don't sting you."

Suddenly Charlene's face lit up. "I know, I know," she called out. "A bee bees an *incest!*"

All the heads nodded.

On the board the teacher wrote the children's conclusion: "A bee is an INSECT."

Stories from Teachers

AN ELEMENTARY SCHOOL TEACHER REPORTED THAT HER CHILDREN responded best to praise and criticism when she used a fanciful description. The following excerpt from her letter illustrates her playful approach.

> To the girl who swiftly finished her math test I said, "You went through all those examples like a mouse nibbling cheese."
>
> To the boy whose composition was difficult to read because he ran one word into the next, I said, "Oh, dear, those poor words are squished together. They look very uncomfortable. But ahhh, look at these two words! They seem very happy. They've got lots of room between each other."
>
> To the child who had difficulty getting his letters on the line, I said, "This *c* is floating in the air, but this one is sitting right on the line. . . . Uh-oh, this *n* is sticking its feet through the floor and the plaster is falling in the neighbor's apartment."
>
> To help all the children during a handwriting exercise, I suggested that they have a "beauty contest" and circle the most beautiful letter on their paper to be the winner. Some children felt they had two equally beautiful letters. In that case both letters were declared "co-winners."

*   *   *

A FIFTH-GRADE TEACHER REPORTED HOW SHE USED DESCRIPTIVE praise when her students were *not* behaving.

> The class was in an "I don't wanna, I'm not gonna" mood. They had endured a solid week of bad

weather and were restless. When we all returned to the room from another indoor recess, the kids continued to play and run around. This is not usually a time when praise is the first thing that comes to mind, but I scanned the class and saw two kids who had settled down and were sitting quietly.

I turned to the chalkboard and wrote their names under the words "Art Time." Then I said to my "model students," "You put your games away immediately when the bell rang. Now you're in your seats ready to see what's next. I appreciate that." The other kids looked at me and then at the two names on the board. A few of them quickly put away their games and hustled to their seats. I added their names to the list and said, "Thank you." Three more sat down.

It was wonderful. I didn't have to raise my voice or issue ultimatums. The kids saw what needed to be done and did it. For those slow to respond, the other students offered loud whispered reminders. But eventually they *all* settled down.

* * *

THIS FINAL STORY SHOWS HOW A GYM TEACHER IN A CITY HIGH school managed to give positive feedback to a rebellious, hostile student without undermining the boy's position with his peers.

Carlos Hernandez did not like to be praised in public. He saw himself as a tough guy who didn't care about school or about what teachers thought. He was admired by the other kids for his defiant attitude. The only time he smiled was when he was being reprimanded for his behavior. Only then did he grin at his peers as if to say "I showed 'em."

During gym class, Albert, one of the less popular students, was having trouble making a basket. Some of the boys were telling him that he "shot like a girl" and others were starting to laugh. Carlos looked at the boys and shook his head.

Greg, the ringleader, said, "What? You like him or something?"

Carlos narrowed his eyes and said one word, "Chill."

They chilled. They didn't say another word. They just shot baskets.

When it was time for the class to head to the locker room, I yelled across the court in a gruff voice, "Hernandez, I want to see you." A few of the boys clustered around the locker room door waiting to see the outcome. I looked over my clipboard at Carlos while turning my back to the other boys. With a stern expression and a low voice I spoke to Carlos.

"Hernandez, I saw what you did for Albert. It takes a strong man to stick up for somebody when others are laughing. You're all right."

Carlos turned and ambled toward the locker room door. The boys who were waiting looked at Carlos's eyes to get a clue of what had happened. Carlos smiled.

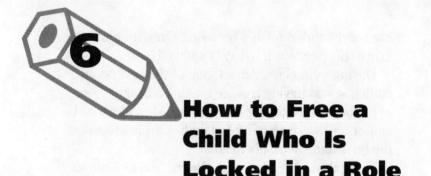

6

How to Free a Child Who Is Locked in a Role

In disbelief I read and reread the letter from the superintendent's office. The words shot through me: "Regret to inform you . . . budget defeat . . . cutbacks . . . transfer to a new school . . . Hemlock Elementary." For the first few weeks of the summer I managed to push the letter out of my mind. But as September grew closer, so did my anxiety at the prospect of starting all over again in a new school. I tried to calm myself. After all, a school was a school. Kids were kids. How different could Hemlock Elementary be? Besides, I had two years of teaching under my belt.

On orientation day I discovered that I wasn't the only teacher in the district who had been reassigned to Hemlock. The assistant principal took all of us newcomers aside and briefed us on the school's disciplinary policies and procedures. His main focus was on the "bad" students and how to "get tough" with them. At the end of the day we were told that we would each be paired up with a mentor teacher, who would help us learn the "right way" to do things at Hemlock. I was glad I had the following day to prepare my classroom. I couldn't listen to one more explanation of the fine points of referral slips, detention, or suspension.

I arrived early the next morning, eager to get organized. On my desk was a class roster with the names of twenty-eight children. I studied the list and noticed that I had eighteen boys and ten girls.

A tall gray-haired woman walked through my door and introduced herself as Mrs. Detner, my assigned mentor. Reaching out her hand for my class list, she said, "I've been teaching at Hemlock for twenty-seven years and I can tell you everything you need to know about these children. I've had them all, and their brothers and sisters—and some of their parents for that matter."

"Does this school have more boys than girls?" I asked as I obediently handed her the list.

She smiled condescendingly. "Not really. You see, being a new teacher, you have to earn the 'good kids'—so to speak."

I informed her that this was my *third* year of teaching, but she cut me off with "Oh, you poor dear, I see you have Mary Ann Ryan. She's a real scatterbrain—completely undependable, no listening skills whatsoever." Shaking her head and clucking her tongue, she continued, "And you've got Angie Milano! That one is sneaky. Can't trust her for a minute. She's full of lies and excuses. . . . And don't tell me they put Joey Simon in your class! He's a very slow learner, has the attention span of a three-year-old. Does nothing but clown around."

I listened, dumbstruck, as she continued working her way down the list. "Now how did Henry Burt get in here? He's an extremely shy child, very nervous, never opens his mouth, but he won't give you any trouble. . . . And neither will Jimmy Potts, except for his dawdling and procrastinating. . . . Oh, but here's Roy Schultz! He'll make up for both of them. Now Roy is smart, but mean—a real bully. And he has very poor impulse control. Just wait until you hear the filth that comes out of his mouth. I can't believe they gave him to someone as sweet looking as you. Oh, well, there's always next year. With a class like this, one can only hope."

She headed for the door and called over her shoulder, "Got loads and loads of work to do. If I finish early, maybe we can talk some more. Or, if nothing else, perhaps we can have lunch together sometime this year."

I nodded politely, but as soon as she was out the door, my head began to ache. What kind of year was I in for? Could she be right about the kids? She made it sound as if their characters and personalities were immutable. Written in stone. Incredible. Hadn't she read any of the studies showing the clear-cut connection between teacher expectation and student performance? Didn't she know that children are capable of change and that a teacher can be a powerful agent of change?

A wave of doubt surged over me. Was I being naive? Foolishly idealistic? Suddenly I remembered a film I had seen years ago in an education course. An elementary school teacher, with a perfectly straight face, told her class that recent research proved that children with brown eyes were smarter than and superior to children with blue eyes. For the rest of the day the children behaved according to the new set of expectations. The brown-eyed children, thrilled by the news, performed better than they ever had in the past. And the blue-eyed children—even the brightest—were so shaken and upset that they couldn't do their work. The following day the teacher, again with a straight face, told the class that an error had been made. In reality blue-eyed children were superior and brown-eyed children were stupid and inferior. Once again the teacher's expectations determined the children's performance. Now it was the blue-eyed children's turn to crow and excel while the brown-eyed children barely functioned, immobilized by shame and self-doubt.

The teacher's methods made me extremely uncomfortable, but there was no denying the results of her experiment. The stark evidence of the power of a teacher to affect a child's self-image for better or worse was forever burned into my brain. I would not fall into the trap of accepting Mrs. Detner's perception of the children. All the kids in my class would have the "right color" eyes.

But was I up to the task ahead? That afternoon as I walked my dog, I found myself thinking about Nicole, a bright, energetic girl in my homeroom last year. I had witnessed firsthand how her teachers, with no malice intended, had little by little cast her in a role.

I heard her gym teacher yell, "Nicole, will you please pipe down! You never shut that mouth of yours!"

I heard her French teacher scold, "Nicole, put your hand down. I *know* you know the answer. Give someone else a chance to talk."

I heard her music teacher say, "Nicole, must you always comment about everything? I'm not interested in what songs *you* think we should sing. Keep your opinions to yourself for a change."

I heard myself say, "Nicole, your talking is disturbing to everyone. Can't you see people are still working on their tests?" Nicole flushed with embarrassment and stopped, but a few minutes later I saw her swing around in her seat and start gabbing with the girl behind her. In exasperation I walked over, took her by the shoulders, and spun her around. "Nicole," I ordered, "stop it! You are a regular talking machine."

By telling her over and over again what was wrong with her, we all assumed that Nicole would listen and improve. She may have listened, but she certainly didn't improve. In fact, she seemed to exhibit even less self-control. It was almost as if she were saying to all of us, "If that's how you see me, then that's how I'll be." Maybe we, her teachers, were responsible for reinforcing her role as "nonstop talker."

Back in the house, I found myself considering Nicole's reaction to our comments from another point of view—a less sympathetic one. Why should the whole burden of changing Nicole's behavior fall upon her teachers' shoulders? Where was Nicole's responsibility in all of this? Why couldn't she have responded to our displeasure and made some small effort to improve?

The phone rang. It was Jane's warm, comforting voice. "We all miss you here," she said. "How's it going over there?"

I couldn't tell her fast enough—about Mrs. Detner and what she had to say about the kids, about my memories of Nicole, and my most recent thoughts about her stubborn defiance.

"Whoa," Jane said. "I'm not at all sure that Nicole was defying you. Isn't it possible that she felt helpless to refute the picture all her teachers were giving her of herself? When you're a kid and you hear everyone say the same thing about you, over and over again, you begin to believe it."

"What makes you so sure?" I asked. There was a long pause. "Jane," I prodded, "tell me."

"Oh . . . I guess I was thinking about me when I was twelve years old and very insecure and what happened my first year away from home at summer camp."

"You had a bad time?"

"No, as a matter of fact, my first summer was wonderful. My bunk mates liked me; my counselor liked me;

even the boys liked me. I learned to swim and to paddle a canoe and won the character award and returned home with a confidence I'd never had before. It was the best summer of my life."

"So all that positive feedback gave you a whole new sense of yourself."

"Now let me tell you what negative feedback can do," Jane continued. "I returned to the same camp the following summer, but nothing was the same. My counselor was new and so were my bunk mates—a boy-crazy, clothes-crazy bunch who decided I was 'immature' and a 'drip.' I tried hard to make friends with them, but the girls drew a tight circle and shut me out. The boys were only interested in the new girls. Even my counselor gave up on me the first time she saw me pitch a ball, and called me a 'klutz.' By the end of the summer I had given up. On the final baseball game of the season, the captains chose up sides and I wasn't picked by either team. I sat on the bench and watched for a while and then walked back to the empty bunk and, for lack of anything better to do, decided to wash my socks. I can still remember watching the suds and dirty water swirl down the sink hole and feeling as if I were going down the hole with the dirty suds. Nobody wanted me. Nobody cared if I lived or died. And there wasn't a thing I could do to change it."

I was silent because I felt for her and didn't know what to say. Finally I asked, "Jane, are you trying to tell me that it's almost impossible to overcome the way other people see you?"

"Maybe some kids are strong enough to hold fast to their own center and to continue to believe in themselves. I wasn't."

Jane changed the subject after that, but when our conversation was over, I couldn't stop thinking about her two

199

summers. Jane seemed like such a strong, self-assured adult that it was hard for me to imagine she was once an insecure kid, vulnerable to the way other people saw her. Then I thought of the children on my class roster that Mrs. Detner had so neatly pigeonholed and wondered about how vulnerable they might be.

When I finally met my fifth-grade class on Monday, I was relieved and pleasantly surprised. Nobody seemed too awful. Basically they looked like any other group of normal kids. But by the end of the first week it occurred to me, more than once, that there might be some truth to Mrs. Detner's characterizations of the children. I pushed that ugly thought aside and determined to continue looking for the best in my students. The last thing they needed from me was another dose of toxic labeling.

By the end of the second week I realized that my good intentions were not enough. For example, when Mary Ann Ryan forgot her ruler *again,* I knew enough not to call her a "scatterbrain," but although I was controlling my tongue, I couldn't seem to control my thoughts. I couldn't stop thinking of her as a "scatterbrain" and heard myself saying things like "Mary Ann, did you remember your lunch money today? . . . Now don't leave your sweater behind again. . . . Be sure to put your assignment pad in your backpack so you don't lose it again."

It's true, I never called her a "scatterbrain," but I was certainly telegraphing how I saw her. And I was doing the same with the other kids as well. I never called Joey Simon a "poor listener," but I did tell him, through clenched teeth, "Joey, *try* to pay attention this time, will you, please?" I never called Jimmy Potts a "dawdler," but I did urge him, "Jimmy, just this once, don't be the last one out of the room." I never told Roy Schultz that he had a foul mouth, but the look I threw him conveyed the message clearly.

I realized that I needed a plan. I sat down that weekend and made a list of the personality traits of my students that bothered me the most. Then I read the chapter in *How to Talk So Kids Will Listen . . .* on how to free children from playing roles and rewrote the summary, substituting the word *students* for *children*.

FREEING STUDENTS FROM PLAYING ROLES

- Look for opportunities to show students a new picture of themselves.
- Put students in situations where they can see themselves differently.
- Let students overhear you say something positive about them.
- Model the behavior you'd like to see.
- Remind students of their past accomplishments.
- State your feelings and/or your expectations.

Here, in cartoon form, are some of the examples I worked out as I imagined applying all the suggestions on my list to the children in my class:

LOOK FOR OPPORTUNITIES TO SHOW STUDENTS A NEW PICTURE OF THEMSELVES

PUT STUDENTS IN SITUATIONS WHERE THEY CAN SEE THEMSELVES DIFFERENTLY

LET STUDENTS OVERHEAR YOU SAY SOMETHING POSITIVE ABOUT THEM

MODEL THE BEHAVIOR YOU'D LIKE TO SEE

REMIND STUDENTS OF THEIR PAST ACCOMPLISHMENTS

BUT WHAT IF A STUDENT PERSISTS IN BEHAVING ACCORDING TO HIS OLD LABEL?
STATE YOUR FEELINGS AND/OR YOUR EXPECTATIONS

I was glad I had made myself figure out what I might actually say to "unlabel" my students, because as a result of that self-imposed exercise, I truly began to think of them differently. And little by little, as I gave them a more positive picture of themselves, I saw changes taking place before my very eyes:

Mary Ann Ryan actually remembered to bring in her signed permission slip for the field trip.

Angie Milano owned up to "borrowing" Mary Ann's ruler.

Henry Burt volunteered an answer!

Joey Simon made a serious contribution to our class discussion.

Jimmy Potts was on time for three days in a row.

Roy Schultz went a whole week without starting a fight. And to everyone's astonishment, in a moment of frustration he banged his fist on the desk and yelled, "*Oh, shoot!*"

I was so excited by what I was seeing, I had to tell someone. Naturally I called Jane. "Every day," I said triumphantly, "I can see these kids letting go of their old roles and exploring new parts of themselves."

Jane was delighted. "I congratulate you," she said, "and now you can congratulate me."

"For what?" I asked.

"For realizing after I spoke to you last time that I'd been casting my own children in roles."

I was shocked. "What are you talking about? What kind of roles? Which children?"

"Mine—Diane and Emily. They're so close in age and so competitive with each other that I wanted each of them to feel how special she was. So I told Diane she's the family artist and Emily that she's the writer in the family. I even threw little Jason into the pot and told him that he was our musician."

"What's wrong with that?" I asked. "Those are all very positive roles."

"That's just the point," Jane said. "Positive or negative, roles are roles. Kids get stuck in them and become fearful about trying any other way of being. Why risk not doing as well as your sister or brother?"

"Or risk doing better," I said, "and having your brother or sister hate you for it."

"Exactly," said Jane. "I want you to know, Liz, that it was your determination to eliminate roles in your classroom that inspired me to try to do the same at home."

On the next two pages you'll see, in cartoon form, what Jane reported as a typical conversation with Diane, followed by Jane's attempts to free her daughter from playing out the role she had given her.

LOCKING A CHILD IN A ROLE

FREEING A CHILD FROM A ROLE

I couldn't stop thinking about those two scenarios after I hung up with Jane. I know that if I were worried about having to write an essay and plagued by the thought that my sister was "the writer in the family," I would take no comfort from my mother's insistence that I was the better artist. Not only would I feel too discouraged even to start my essay, but I'd probably think, "If it's my 'art' that gives me value in my family, what would happen if I ever stopped being good at it? Or if one day my sister brought home a beautiful drawing? Where would that leave *me?*"

But if I put myself in the second scene, where my mother focused only on me and pointed out my unique powers, I'd feel very different. I'd think, "Maybe I *could* tackle that essay. Maybe there *were* things I had to say about justice." It wouldn't even matter whether my sister was a good writer or a bad writer. She could be any kind of writer she cared to be. And I would be free to be me.

So much to think about. I was clear in a way I had never been before. My role as teacher and Jane's role as parent *was to be fierce about not permitting roles at all. No more labeling of children's characters. Every child* needs to be seen as a multifaceted being—now shy and withdrawn, now boisterous and outgoing; now slow and thoughtful, now swift and purposeful; now stubborn and uncooperative, now flexible. But never the same, always in process, always with the capacity for change and growth.

No more labeling of academic ability—"above average" . . . "below average" . . . "mediocre" . . . "brilliant" . . . "slow." *Every child* needs to be seen as a "learner" and encouraged to experience the joy of intellectual discovery and the satisfaction of making progress—however fast or slow.

No more singling out children with rare artistic or ath-

letic gifts and showering them with attention at the expense of their less talented siblings or classmates. Yes, the gifted few need recognition and nurturing, but so do *all* children. *Every child* needs to be encouraged to experience the pleasures of sports, song, dance, theater, and art without worrying about having to be the star athlete or a musical genius or the class actress or the family artist.

No more imprisoning of children's hopes and dreams and possibilities by locking them in with labels. Who knows what any of us might become if just one person believed in us enough to help us explore our unexplored selves.

FREEING A CHILD FROM PLAYING A ROLE
At Home and in School

Adult: Nicole, you're a "motor mouth." No one can get a word in edgewise with you.

Instead of the above:

1. LOOK FOR OPPORTUNITIES TO SHOW THE CHILD A NEW PICTURE OF HERSELF.

"What self-control! Even though you had a lot more to say, you realized that others needed a chance to talk."

2. PUT THE CHILD IN A SITUATION WHERE SHE CAN SEE HERSELF DIFFERENTLY.

"Nicole, I'd like you to chair the (class/family) meeting and make sure that everyone gets a turn to speak."

3. LET THE CHILD OVERHEAR YOU SAY SOMETHING POSITIVE ABOUT HER.

"Nicole has so many wonderful ideas that it's hard for her to hold back. Nevertheless I've seen her do it."

4. MODEL THE BEHAVIOR YOU'D LIKE TO SEE.

"Oh, I'm sorry. I didn't mean to interrupt. Please finish what you were saying. My thought will keep."

5. REMIND THE CHILD OF HER PAST ACCOMPLISHMENTS.

"I remember the discussion we had on capital punishment. You listened quietly, but when you finally gave your views, some people changed their position."

6. STATE YOUR FEELINGS AND/OR EXPECTATIONS.

"Nicole, when other people are waiting to speak, I'd like you to keep your comments brief."

Questions and Stories from Parents and Teachers

Questions from Parents

1. When we encourage children to stop playing roles—like "the big boss" or "the critic" or "Mr. Stubborn" or "Miss Sensitive"—isn't there the danger that something good about the role will be lost along with the bad?

Anytime we help a child risk another way of behaving, we have to make sure that we support whatever might be positive about the role he has been playing. The "big boss" needs to be appreciated for his leadership qualities. The "critic" needs to be commended for her powers of observation. "Mr. Stubborn" needs respect for his persistence and determination. "Miss Sensitive" needs recognition for her caring heart.

2. I'm trying to help my son change his role from undependable to dependable. Now I'm wondering if I'm not taking him out of one role and putting him into another. What do you think?

It's important that we not cast children in any role. It would feel just as threatening to a youngster to be told "You're *always* so dependable" as it would be for him to hear "I can *never* depend upon you." Instead point out to your son one instance in which he behaved dependably: "You said you'd take responsibility for finding out the cost

216

of your lost book, and you did." That tells him that when *he chooses* to be dependable, he can.

3. I still don't see the harm in telling a child, "You're always so dependable." Wouldn't that give him something to live up to?

By telling a child he's *always* anything, you back him into a tight corner. He can either behave undependably in order to prove you wrong, or he can take on the new role given him—no matter what the circumstances or inner cost ("My ankle still isn't healed, but I can't let my team down"). We want our children to be free of such constraints—to be able to evaluate each situation as it arises and make a decision based upon their best judgment—not someone else's view of how they should *always* behave.

4. Is there anything you can do when one child labels another? I'm thinking of my daughter, Wendy, who calls her friend Susan "mean and selfish" whenever they play together and Susan doesn't give her what she wants.

Never underestimate your power as a parent to influence the children in your care. When one child labels another, you can intervene to help them both see the best in each other: "Wendy, I know you ask for what you want *without* calling Susan a name. She can be generous when you approach her in another way."

Stories from Parents

T<small>HIS</small> <small>FIRST STORY WAS FROM THE MOTHER OF A</small> "<small>FORGETFUL</small>" child.

My daughter, Polly, is the original absentminded professor. When it's time for her to do her homework, I discover that either she hasn't brought her book home or that she lost her assignment sheet, or that she remembered her book but doesn't remember what pages she's supposed to do. Even her grandmother, who adores her, says she'd forget her head if it weren't attached to her shoulders.

I've tried everything—being patient, yelling, giving her long lectures on responsibility. Nothing works. My husband keeps telling me that I'm only making things worse and giving Polly a poor self-image. Last week I got so annoyed with him, I said, "Fine. You take over." And he did.

For instance, when Polly asked me for three dollars for her field trip, I didn't make a big deal about how she lost her money last time. I just told her to speak to her father. He didn't have any singles, so he gave her a five-dollar bill and said, "I expect you to bring home two dollars in change. Just figure out a safe place to keep your money until you can give it to me." She did! She put it in her shoe and gave him his change when he got home that evening.

About an hour later she went into a panic because she couldn't find her assignment book. My husband said, "Polly, when you can listen, I have a question for you." She immediately said, "What?"

He said, "Who do you know in your class who would have the assignment?"

218

She said, "Cindy," and went right into the kitchen and made a phone call. Later, when my husband went into her room to say good night, he gave the two dollars back to her and told her to buy herself the biggest assignment book she could find for the money and to write something on the cover that would help her to remember to bring it home.

She said, "Like what?"

He said, "Any little smartie-pie who could think of keeping her money in her shoe can figure out something to write."

She said, "I know. I'll write 'Don't Forget Me, Smartie-Pie.'" Then she giggled.

I have to admit I think my husband is on the right track.

*   *   *

THIS NEXT STORY SHOWS A STEPMOTHER MOVING IN TO PROTECT her stepdaughters from being cast in roles by unthinking relatives.

I recently married a man who has nonidentical twin girls. At our Thanksgiving dinner I heard their uncle jokingly refer to them as the "beauty" and the "brain." It is true that one is unusually pretty and the other is an honor student, but still I was horrified.

I turned to look at the girls to see their reaction. Neither one of them seemed surprised. Evidently they had heard him say it before. An aunt tried to change the subject, but I was so upset, I couldn't let it go. In a loud voice I said, "I've known Joy and Ellen for almost a year now and I can tell you, as someone who has lived with them, they are *both* endowed with superior intelligence. And to me they're *both* strong in the beauty department."

I may not have endeared myself to the uncle, but I could see by the expressions on the girls' faces that they were glad I had spoken up.

*   *   *

A PARENT VOLUNTEER REPORTED THIS NEXT EXPERIENCE.

I was assigned to a third-grade class of racially mixed and mostly very poor children. Many of their parents were migrant workers. The teacher took me aside on my first day and told me I would be working with Billy and Jonathan, age nine. Then she briefed me on their backgrounds: Billy came from a home of drugs and violence. Jonathan lived with his grandmother because his father was in jail. She warned me not to expect too much from them: "They both like to make trouble and they're not too bright. As a matter of fact, in this school"—she paused here and lowered her voice—"they call children like these 'throwaways.' "

I couldn't get over what she'd said. Throwaways? Disposable children? Human garbage? Those were "fightin' words" for me! I started my first reading lesson with the boys with the determination to do right by them. They yawned in my face. Billy told me he'd watched a late-night movie that ended at two A.M. and Jonathan said he was hungry. I found out later he'd had no breakfast.

The next day I brought snacks to school for both boys and they ate while I read them a story. Then I gave them each a book with riddles and jokes and asked them to choose one to read aloud. Jonathan picked a joke about a farmer and his pig. I laughed at the punch line. Then Billy asked, "Can I read mine?" He read haltingly, but he seemed to understand the content.

That day broke the ice for us. I continued bringing snacks and working with them on their reading and math. Little by little I realized the teacher was wrong. They *were* bright—both of them. Jonathan read with excellent comprehension and Billy was good with numbers. I never missed an opportunity to let them know how impressed I was by their rapid progress and what a pleasure it was to work with them. It wasn't put on. I really fell in love with those two kids.

After a few months they were reading and doing math on grade level and behaving cooperatively in class. I felt vindicated. I knew it was because I treated these so-called throwaways as important, respected children whom I treasured.

A few weeks before the term was over, Billy's family was evicted and he had to leave school. When he came to class on his last day, he seemed sad and withdrawn. I told him I'd be sure to get his address from his new school so that Jonathan and I could write to him. Then I hugged him good-bye and told him I'd never forget him.

In the days that followed I found myself missing Billy terribly and wishing I could have had more time with him and wondering how long his better feelings about himself would last in a cold, rejecting world.

Questions from Teachers

1. I've been told that on the first day of school I should inform my students of the rules and the consequences for not obeying them—name on board, loss of recess privileges, call to parent, after-school detention, etc., all the way to suspension. Now I'm wondering if this approach doesn't put the kids in the roles of "troublemakers" and send them the message that I expect them to misbehave. What do you think?

Students tend to live up or down to their teachers' expectations. If you see them as faulty people who need to be fixed up and straightened out, they'll supply you with plenty of work. If instead you choose to look for whatever is positive and build on that, they'll work equally hard to justify your faith in them.

One teacher reported that she starts the term by describing some of the more exciting projects she has in mind (for example, a class radio station), makes it clear that she'll need everyone's input and involvement, and then, pointing to a list on the bulletin board, says, "Now let's go over a few rules that will help us to accomplish our goals. You probably know most of them already."

"That," she says, "lets my students know, right from the beginning, that I see them as basically responsible, cooperative, creative people who have something of value to contribute to their class."

2. What can you do if, despite your best efforts, a student persists in playing out a role?

Persevere. Don't take the child's resistance personally. The youngster who continues to act out a negative role isn't necessarily out to "get you." Chances are he's clinging to what is safe and familiar. He may need many repetitions of your new words and your new attitude before he can begin to trust you or to trust himself to experiment with new behaviors.

3. In the neighborhood in which I teach, the whole environment is so violent, some of the teachers seem to accept as fact the idea that these are "junior delinquents" who will be mean and rough with each other—even in their play—and that there's not much anybody can do about it. I'm wondering if you agree.

The view you describe can be dangerous. When we adults stand by silently and allow children to hurt each other, in the name of play, we sanction a form of violence that can spill over into all of their relationships. We need to treat children not as they are, but as we hope they will become. One teacher who was deeply disturbed by the way her students callously hurt each other, both physically and verbally, reported that she was determined to help them see themselves as people who *could* be sensitive to each other's feelings. When their horseplay became too rough, she'd intervene with "Hey, that can hurt! One way to tell if you're hurting someone is to look at his face. Does he seem upset? Is he crying? That will tell you you've gone too far."

Once, at recess, she spotted a couple of kids holding down another in what had started out as a playful wrestling match. The boy who was pinned down was getting frantic, but the others kept laughing and piling on. When she tried to stop them, the boys protested that they weren't fighting. They were just "playing and having fun."

She replied, "In a play fight *everyone* should be having fun. You need to ask the boy on the bottom if *he's* still having fun. If he isn't, it's got to stop." In summary, she said, "I want my students to know that I won't allow them to brutalize or be brutalized while I'm around."

4. Aren't children born with real personality differences? I've noticed that some of my students really are more impulsive or shy or aggressive than others. They're not playing out an assigned role.

Just because a child is born with a particular genetic predisposition doesn't mean he has to be trapped by it. The "impulsive" child needs help and practice in slowing down and considering the consequences of his actions; the "shy" child needs to experience the pleasure of reaching out to others; the "aggressive" child needs to learn how to relate to others peacefully. We need to help all children become all that they can be.

A Story from a Teacher

THE FOLLOWING EXPERIENCE SHOWS WHAT CAN HAPPEN WHEN A teacher is determined to see a student in a new light.

> Darryl Jackson was a large, obnoxious ten-year-old, twice as big as anyone else in my class. Because of his size you expected him to be more mature, but he behaved like a big, loud, goofy fool. He'd bop the other kids on the head, shove them, fling himself around, run out into the hall yelling "Arrghh!" if he heard someone coming. Anything to get attention. If that didn't work, he'd start talking in a loud voice about "titties" and "doo-doo."

The kids didn't like him, either. He was always putting them down: "You didn't know *that?* You're stupid!" On the bus for a school trip, he'd insist on taking up two seats for himself. In the lunchroom he'd gobble his sandwich and stick out his tongue with half-chewed food still on it and laugh.

I found myself saying his name over and over again with increasing annoyance: "Darryl, stop it! . . . Darryl, be quiet!" Sometimes I'd physically push him back into his seat: "Darryl, I said, 'SIT DOWN!!' " The underlying message in my voice was "I don't like you. . . . Your very presence annoys me. . . . You are my *irritant!*"

Once, I became so exasperated with him I made a gesture of tearing my hair out. Darryl's eyes lit up with pleasure. With a big grin he said, "I'm driving you crazy, right, Mrs. Bergen?" He had achieved his goal. And not only with me. Every teacher in the school knew his name and they all hated him. At the lunch table they'd trade Darryl stories. He had succeeded in making himself famous throughout the school. It was almost funny in a horrible sort of way.

He was so disruptive that I considered consulting the guidance counselor or the school psychologist about him. But there was a stubborn little part of me that decided to "take him on" myself. I knew that if there was going to be any small possibility of Darryl changing, I would have to change my tactics. But I also realized that I couldn't just do it mechanically. I had to find at least one quality in Darryl that I genuinely liked or admired. Without some real feeling for the child, the whole process would be an exercise in manipulation. Maybe that would be better than nothing, but I was hoping for more.

The next day I watched Darryl like a hawk. His one saving grace was that he was talented at drawing. He could look at any object and reproduce it accurately. I saw Felix call him over to show him his drawing. Felix has poor hand-eye coordination and his drawing was barely decipherable. Nevertheless, he pointed to his squiggly lines and told Darryl, "Look, here's the man about to shoot the dinosaur."

I thought Darryl would make fun of him, but instead he just smiled good-naturedly and pointed to the squiggles and said encouraging things like "Yeah, and here's an alien coming down in a spaceship." That touched me. So Darryl could be sweet. Even generous! Maybe it was because he felt so secure in the area of art.

From that moment on I launched my "campaign of positivity." I started by choosing Darryl for small tasks like cleaning the chalkboard or putting away the *World Books* in alphabetical order or feeding the turtle, and then thanking him for helping me. It turned out that Darryl liked animals. I put him in charge of the hamsters for the week and told him that the animals seemed to love it when he held them because he was so gentle. He beamed.

Then I went to work on helping the other kids in the class see him differently. Whenever someone needed help, I'd say, "Oh, get Darryl to show you how that works. He's good at fractions." Or "Darryl, you know a lot about animals. What kind of dog would make a good watchdog?" I was hoping they'd think since the teacher didn't see him as a pest anymore, maybe he wasn't.

Whenever I absolutely *had* to reprimand him, I

tried to preface it with something positive: "Darryl, I know how hard it is to wait, but Felix needs to finish what he's saying." Or "Darryl, I know it isn't easy to control the urge to get out of your seat, but right now I need everyone sitting down and paying attention." After a while Darryl started saying things like "See, Mrs. Bergen, I'm controlling myself!" Or "See, I waited my turn." Or "I wanted to jump up, but I didn't." And I'd always respond quickly and warmly, "I noticed that." Or "That was hard to do."

Then I started writing short notes to his mother:

> Dear Mrs. Jackson,
> Darryl has been in charge of our class pets this month and all the animals are clean, well fed, and happy.
> > Sincerely,
> > Mrs. Bergen

Darryl loved that. He asked me to tell his other teachers about him now. I was happy to oblige: "Mrs. Kramer, Darryl drew a map of the United States and filled in all the states and capitals."

From these small changes in my behavior came large changes in Darryl's. He became very affectionate toward me. He stopped annoying, shoving, and teasing the other kids. He was always jumping up to help someone draw or read or carry. When his new friend, Felix, had no money for a class trip, Darryl became despondent and later in the week lent him the money. He became a team player. The enemy of everyone became the friend of everyone. He shared his sandwich, candy, anything. He was Mr. Sociability. He was still loud and abrasive, but now those qualities were combined and tempered with socially desirable traits.

The other teachers became aware of Darryl's feelings for me and used it to control his behavior. They'd say, "If you don't stop that, I'll tell Mrs. Bergen," and he'd stop on a dime. He didn't want anything bad about him to get back to me.

But in the end his new behavior never did carry over to the other teachers. They still didn't like him, and he wasn't going to go out of his way to be cooperative or pleasant with people who treated him like a big nuisance. You couldn't intimidate Darryl into behaving better if he felt you didn't care. You had to appreciate him to get appreciation from him.

The Parent-Teacher Partnership

IT HAD BEEN A HARD DAY. THE ACCUMU-
LATED TENSION AND EXCITEMENT OF MEETING ONE PARENT AFTER
another had left me drained. And I still had a long
evening of conferences ahead. No time to go home. I
drove to a small restaurant in town, hoping to have a
quiet, relaxing dinner before the next wave of parents.

The man who parked his car in the space next to mine
looked familiar. As soon as he stepped into the light, I rec-
ognized him. "Ken," I called out, "I'm so glad to see you
again! What are you doing here?"

Ken grinned at me broadly. "Probably the same thing
you are. I've got three more conferences scheduled
tonight and I need to refuel. How about sitting together? I
want to hear how they're treating you at Hemlock."

So much for my quiet dinner. Once inside we looked
around the crowded restaurant for an empty table. There
were none. A voice behind a waving hand called, "Liz!
Over here!" It was Julie, a friend from my high school
days who had moved away years ago, and her older sister,
Martha.

"Don't look so surprised," Julie said. "I'm here for a few
days visiting Martha. Come join us."

I gestured in Ken's direction, trying to indicate that the

two of us were together. Julie nodded, pointed to two empty chairs at her table, and beckoned to both of us.

The first part of our conversation was an exchange of introductions and catch-up. It seemed that Julie was now a single mom, doing well on her own, and "the baby" was now six. Martha's oldest boy was a teenager. I explained that Ken and I were former colleagues and that I'd been transferred to a new school, that he was still at the old school, and that we were both on a break between conferences.

"Parent-teacher conferences?" Julie said with distaste. "I've got one coming up next week and I am *not* looking forward to it."

That seemed like a strange thing to say. After we ordered dinner, I said, "Sounds as if you might have had a bad experience at your last conference."

Julie rolled her eyes and sighed.

I was curious but didn't want to pry. Ken had no such compunctions. "Why? What went wrong?"

"I don't know if you'd understand," Julie said nervously. "You're not a mother."

"I would admit to that," said Ken. "But try me anyway."

Julie paused a moment. Then she said, "I don't know if I can explain this but . . . look, I think my daughter, Becky, is a great kid, but when I went to my last conference and the teacher told me, with this phony little laugh, 'Well, to be perfectly frank, Becky is just a *bit* disorganized, and she doesn't always *quite* tell the truth,' I felt sick inside. And later when I went home, I began to look at Becky differently and to wonder if she had me fooled and if she really was sneaky and disorganized."

I was dismayed by Julie's experience. "That's terrible," I said. "You left the conference doubting your own child."

"And I probably shouldn't even be saying this," Julie

went on, "but teachers have a way of making me feel as if anything wrong with my child is my fault. If only I 'did this' or 'did that' or spent more time with her or were a better parent, Becky would be a better child. . . . And this may sound silly altogether, but sometimes I get this feeling that some teachers think they're superior to me because they have a college education and I don't."

Ken raised his eyebrows. "Oh, come now," he said derisively.

"Don't dismiss what Julie's trying to tell you," Martha said, jabbing the air with her finger. "I have a college degree and I also happen to be the vice president of my firm. But I remember very well how it feels to be put in one of those little kid's seats across from the teacher's desk and having to sit there while she tells me about my son's poor listening skills. In less than a minute I'm reduced to a scared little girl again being scolded by the teacher."

"Wait a second," I said. "I'm getting confused. That's not my idea of what a conference ought to be—with the teacher doing all the talking and telling you what's wrong with your child. No. To me a conference is a two-way street. We teachers want input from you parents. We need it. That's the purpose of the conference. We welcome your ideas."

"Really," Martha said disdainfully. "Then how come I feel as if I have to walk on eggs before daring to make the smallest suggestion? Because if, heaven forbid, I happen to offend the teacher by hinting she do something differently, and she gets angry at me, I know darn well she'll take it out on my kid."

"Martha, that's not fair," I protested, "and it's not even true!"

Martha ignored me. "But what really gets me," she

continued, "is when teachers use this patronizing tone. 'The problem with Michael is blah, blah, blah. I know you work, but maybe if you could spend a little more time with him. . . .' Or 'If Michael doesn't start paying attention now, he'll never make it in the next grade.' And the one that always leaves me feeling guilty and inadequate is 'I'm sorry to tell you, your son is not living up to his potential.'"

I was stunned by Martha's comments and embarrassed. I'd said those very words to a parent this afternoon. My first impulse was to launch into a long defense of myself and all my colleagues, but I decided to take another tack. "Is there anything else that bothers you?" I asked calmly.

Martha pounced on my question. "Yes! I hate it when they use teacher mumbo-jumbo that makes you feel like an idiot. 'If you want Michael to decode phonemes and consonant blends (translation: read), then you need to spend an hour every night helping him with his reading program.'"

"And," Julie added, "what parent has an hour a night after working all day and shopping and cleaning? I know that by the time I've fixed dinner and done the dishes and the laundry and gotten Becky into her pajamas, I'm too tired to do anything but read her one bedtime story."

Martha nodded in agreement. "But what really galls me," she said, "is that teachers feel no sense of responsibility to communicate with parents. I never hear from them until the problem is so serious that it would take a miracle to fix it, like when Michael was in junior high and he stopped doing his social studies homework. The teacher couldn't be bothered to inform me of that fact until the week before report cards came out. How's a kid supposed to make up fifteen assignments in one week?"

This was more than I could take. "Hold on," I said. "Everything you say may be so, but please understand, teachers can have over thirty kids in a class with each one needing attention. It's unrealistic to expect a personal call every time a student falls behind in his work."

Very coolly, Ken asked, "What exactly is it that you parents want from teachers?"

Martha looked directly into Ken's eyes. "Respect," she said. "I'd like teachers to treat me and my child with the same respect they want for themselves."

I could see the color rising in Ken's face. "Respect?" he snapped. "What kind of respect do teachers get? Everybody dumps on us. We're held responsible for everything that goes wrong and we get it from all sides. Parents complain about us; the kids are rude; the principal demands that we fit more and more into the curriculum; the administration pushes us to be more creative as they cut our budget for the most basic supplies; colleges are dissatisfied with us because the kids aren't prepared to do college-level work; and business indicts us for sending them graduates who aren't qualified for the work world. But does anyone really support education? Is anyone willing to pay teachers what they deserve? The people in this community didn't even vote for the last bond issue."

Julie was openmouthed. The people at the next table had turned to stare at us. I was very uncomfortable. This time Ken had gone too far. But Martha was undaunted by Ken's outburst. "Well, I voted *for* the bond issue," she said forcefully, "and if it were up to me, you teachers would have gotten a big raise in salary and all the money you need to buy all the supplies you need. But what Julie and I are trying to say is that we parents feel disrespected and shut out of our children's education. It's true, we don't have your professional expertise, but we have a lot to contribute—if you'd let us. We *want* to help!"

"Parents help?" Ken exploded. "Like the ones who can't even be bothered to come to a conference because they'll miss their favorite TV show? Or the ones who are too drunk or stoned to even care? Or the parents who think nothing of keeping an older kid out of school to take care of a younger one? Or the parents who pressure us to give their kids A's because Mommy and Daddy are determined to get them into an Ivy League school?"

Martha didn't back down. "Ken," she said, "you're making an unfair case against parents." She turned to me for support. "Liz, has that been your experience?"

I desperately wanted to lower the heat on this conversation, but Martha was asking for the truth and suddenly I needed to tell it. "Not exactly," I said. "I've had parents who were a joy to work with, but there are some with whom I would hesitate to bring up a problem. I told one father that his son was disruptive and that night he got a beating. And right now I have a couple who are in the middle of a custody fight. It's obvious to me that their child has some serious problems, but during the conference all they did was blame each other and try to get me to take sides. . . . I guess parents are under so much stress today and in so much pain in their personal lives that it's hard for them to focus on their kids. I find I have to listen to them and their problems before they can even begin to talk about any problems their children might have."

Martha threw up her hands. "I give up," she said. "According to you two, we parents are a self-centered, irresponsible, pathetic bunch."

"Don't take it personally," Ken said. "We're just letting off steam. Of course there are wonderful parents out there. They do their best and then some. What you're hearing are the ravings of two frustrated teachers who care very much about your kids and who are upset because they don't always get the support they need from parents."

Everyone fell silent. Very tentatively Julie said, "I guess whenever I go to a conference, I worry about what the teacher will have to say about my child. It never occurs to me to think about what the teacher might feel or need."

"Well, in all fairness, maybe we should think about it," Martha conceded. "Liz, what exactly would you want from us parents?"

Her question caught me by surprise. I thought a moment and said, "Honest information—about how your child does at home, his interests, his worries . . . anything you could tell me that would help me to understand him better. And I guess if there are any problems, I'd want the parent to be willing to think along with me and work with me so we can end up doing what's best for the child."

Martha nodded her head approvingly. "And how about you, Ken? What do you want?"

"Feedback," Ken said. "I want to know which—if any— of my daily efforts on your kid's behalf is having an impact. What does he have to say about school? Or about me? Without some feedback, it's hard to make an intelligent decision about what he needs more of or less of."

"I don't disagree with that," Martha said.

Ken sat back in his chair and extended his arm in a courtly gesture. "Okay, Martha, the floor is all yours. You've had a few choice things to say about teachers. Suppose I turn your question back to you. What exactly would you parents want from us?"

Martha furrowed her brow. Then, speaking slowly, she said, "To me, what's most important is to leave the conference with something I can hang on to. Some picture of my child that helps me feel good about him. I don't think teachers have any idea of the power they have or the effect of their words. Most parents have experience with only a handful of children. Teachers have hundreds of children over the course of their careers. A teacher's view of a child carries enormous weight with parents. When a teacher tells you your child is exceptional in any way—good or bad—you take it seriously. And you take the words home with you.

"I remember how irritated and disgusted I was with Michael when he was in preschool because he was so whiny and clingy and not independent and outgoing like the other four-year-olds. But the day I had a conference with his teacher, everything changed for me. She beamed at me with pleasure and said, 'I'm so happy to meet Michael's mother. He is such an unusually warm and loving little boy.' Her words went inside me like a light. I had never thought of him that way before. That picture she gave me of my son rang true for me and helped me through more times than she'll ever know."

I was touched by Martha's story. I turned to Julie and put my hand on her arm. "How about you?" I asked. "What would you like from a parent conference, Julie?"

"I'd like to leave with something I can tell my child that will give her more confidence in herself. . . . Something I can repeat to Becky when she looks up at me with her big eyes and asks, 'What did the teacher say about me?' "

The rest of our dinner hour went by swiftly as we spoke honestly and shared what was most important to each of us in our role as parent or teacher and how we envisioned the ideal conference—first from the parent's perspective and then from the teacher's perspective.

On the following pages you'll find, in cartoon form, the essence of what we said.

THE IDEAL CONFERENCE: A PARENT'S PERSPECTIVE

INSTEAD OF STARTING WITH WHAT'S WRONG,

START BY TELLING ME SOMETHING RIGHT ABOUT MY CHILD.

INSTEAD OF LISTING MY CHILD'S LIMITATIONS,

POINT OUT WHAT HE NEEDS TO DO.

INSTEAD OF TELLING ME WHAT TO DO,

DESCRIBE WHAT HAS WORKED AT SCHOOL.

THE IDEAL CONFERENCE: A PARENT'S PERSPECTIVE

INSTEAD OF GIVING UP ON MY CHILD,

DEVELOP A PLAN WITH ME.

INSTEAD OF FORGETTING THE PLAN,

FOLLOW THROUGH AFTER THE CONFERENCE.

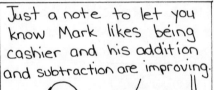

INSTEAD OF VIOLATING MY CONFIDENCE,

KEEP MY PERSONAL LIFE PERSONAL.

THE IDEAL CONFERENCE: A TEACHER'S PERSPECTIVE

INSTEAD OF STARTING WITH WHAT'S WRONG,

START BY DESCRIBING SOMETHING RIGHT.

INSTEAD OF ATTACKING ME,

DESCRIBE WHAT YOUR CHILD NEEDS.

INSTEAD OF WITHHOLDING INFORMATION,

SHARE PERTINENT INFORMATION.

THE IDEAL CONFERENCE: A TEACHER'S PERSPECTIVE

INSTEAD OF TELLING ME WHAT TO DO,

SHARE WHAT HAS WORKED AT HOME.

INSTEAD OF REFUSING TO COOPERATE,

HELP TO DEVELOP A PLAN.

INSTEAD OF FORGETTING THE PLAN,

FOLLOW THROUGH AFTER THE CONFERENCE.

After sharing our different versions of the ideal conference, we realized how remarkably similar our needs were.

- Both parents and teachers need appreciation, information, and understanding from one another.
- We both need to have our efforts acknowledged.
- We both need respect.
- We both need to work together, and to support each other, and to look for the best in each other, so that we can give that best to our children.

When it was time to go, we exchanged good-byes reluctantly. I think we were all feeling the enormity of the emotional journey we had taken in the short hour we had spent together. We had started out at opposite poles. It was parents against teachers. Us against them. Yet by the time we were ready to part company, we were all in the same place, on the same team, bound together by our common commitment to our children's progress and our determination never to give up on any child.

THE IDEAL CONFERENCE

Instead of starting with what's wrong . . .
1. START BY DESCRIBING SOMETHING RIGHT.

> *Teacher:* I enjoy Sam's thoughtful questions.
> *Parent:* Sam liked the lesson you gave on rockets.

Instead of pointing out what the child hasn't done . . .
2. DESCRIBE WHAT THE CHILD NEEDS TO DO.

> *Teacher:* Sam needs to make up all the work he missed the week he was out sick.
> *Parent:* I think he's feeling overwhelmed. He can probably use some extra help to catch up.

Instead of withholding information . . .
3. SHARE PERTINENT INFORMATION.

> *Parent:* He used to play outdoors when he got home. Now he just sits in front of the TV.
> *Teacher:* I see him yawning a lot lately in class.

Instead of giving each other advice . . .
4. DESCRIBE WHAT HAS WORKED AT HOME OR IN SCHOOL.
> *Parent:* Ever since he's been sick, he seems to do better if he takes a short break every fifteen or twenty minutes.
> *Teacher:* I notice he has more energy after recess.

Instead of giving up on the child . . .
5. DEVELOP A PLAN TOGETHER.

> *Teacher:* I'll ask another student to help Sam with the work he missed. And I'll see to it that he takes more frequent breaks.
>
> *Parent:* And I'll make sure he watches less TV and gets some fresh air and exercise.

Instead of ending on a negative note . . .
6. END THE CONFERENCE WITH A POSITIVE STATEMENT THAT CAN BE REPEATED TO THE CHILD.

> *Teacher:* Tell Sam I have confidence that he'll be able to make up all his work. Also tell him that I enjoy having him in my class.
>
> *Parent:* I will. I know he'll be glad to hear that.

Instead of forgetting the plan after the conference . . .
7. FOLLOW THROUGH WITH THE PLAN.

> *Teacher:* Jeffrey has been helping Sam and he's almost all caught up. He also seems to have more energy lately.
>
> *Parent:* My husband has started jogging and Sam has been joining him.

Questions and Stories from Parents and Teachers

Questions from Parents

1. Is it ever a good idea for a child to be present at a conference? Sometimes I think my son might benefit from being there.

At the beginning of the conference both you and the teacher will need the freedom to talk to each other openly without having to worry about the effect your words might have upon your son. In the meantime he can wait outside the room, read in the library, or play on the playground.

However, at one point it may be useful to invite him in to be a part of the conference. Be aware of his vulnerable position. At his tender age he must now deal with two of the most powerful, significant adults in his life—at the same time! It will help if you can start by sharing with him the most positive information you've exchanged thus far. For example:

Parent: I've been telling Mrs. Fisher how much the whole family has learned from you about the rain forest, ever since you started on your project.

Teacher: And I've been telling your mother how much all the children enjoyed the pictures you brought in—especially the one of the red-eyed tree frog.

245

The conference could end there. But suppose there is something that needs improvement? Suppose your son procrastinates or has trouble organizing his work? Either you or the teacher can broach the problem.

> *Teacher:* There's still a lot of work to be done before you give your final presentation to the class. Let's talk about how to go about it.

From there on in the three of you can discuss how to organize and schedule the many steps involved in completing a class project. Ideally the teacher might say: "Think it would help if I set some additional smaller deadlines for you, like when to turn in your note cards and your outline and the first draft of your report?"

Ideally you might add: "Would it help if I dropped you off at the library a few afternoons this week so you could start your research?"

Ideally your son would volunteer: "Maybe I could write down everything I have to do and put a date next to it and then check off each thing after I do it."

You'll know the three-way conference has succeeded if your child leaves feeling hopeful and motivated.

2. My daughter, Mia, is on the shy side. Last year she had a teacher who encouraged friendships in her class. This year she has a new teacher and is in a class with mostly new children. She doesn't complain, but I know she's lonely and unhappy. What's the best way to approach her teacher to enlist her help?

Be prepared. Do some thinking in advance about what the teacher might do to help your daughter connect with other children. Is there a class activity Mia could be part of—a play or an art project? Is there some responsibility she might share with another child—hall monitor or co-editor of the class newspaper? And be sure to ask if there is anything *you* can do to help—either with the play or paper or art project. Don't press for an immediate response. The teacher will need time to consider your thoughts and possibly come up with some of her own.

3. At my last conference the teacher told me that my son, Tony, was lazy and uncooperative. I was very upset but didn't know how to respond. If it ever happens again, is there anything I can do?

It's important to be armed with a pencil and paper when you go to a conference. If the teacher says anything negative about your child, you can inquire as to what specific behavior caused him to make his judgment: "Lazy? Could you tell me what you mean by that?"

Suppose the teacher answers, "He's the only one in the art class who leaves dirty brushes and open containers of paint behind him." As you write, say aloud, "Tony needs to clean his brushes and screw the caps back on the paint jars before he leaves the art room."

Suppose the teacher persists and says, "And he's also uncooperative." Ask again, "Can you tell me what he does that makes you say that?"

If the teacher answers, "He never shuts his mouth during silent reading," again, say aloud as you write, "Tony needs to control his urge to talk during silent reading."

By translating the teacher's negative comments into a statement of *what needs to be done,* you will help point the teacher, yourself, and your son in a more positive direction.

4. This year my daughter, Lisa, who has been in special ed, was mainstreamed into a regular class. Her teacher believes in making heavy demands upon his students and has always had great success with them. He's convinced it's because of his high expectations. Lisa is a hard worker, but she's barely keeping up. Her teacher is irritated with her and she's becoming very discouraged. What can I do?

Our expectations should be strong but realistic. We do a terrible disservice to children when we insist that they can do what they're not capable of doing and urge them to "try harder." A child who hasn't mastered addition or subtraction won't be able to do multiplication or division, no matter how strong her teacher's expectations. If Lisa is overwhelmed by her teacher's demands, then you need to help him understand her present academic abilities and encourage him to break down his large goals for her into smaller, *doable* tasks so that she can experience success, *one step at a time.*

5. My son came home from school the other day looking very agitated. He said that his teacher hated him. I wasn't sure how to respond. What would you suggest?

After you acknowledge his distress, listen to what he has to tell you. Sometimes the problem can be quickly pinpointed and eased: "Oh, so you were embarrassed when she yelled at you in front of everyone for taking the stapler from her drawer. You wish she had called you over and told you quietly. . . . And I'll bet you wish you had thought to ask for permission first."

If your son can't give you a clear picture of what's going on in school and continues to complain that his teacher hates him, then you need to speak to the teacher. Chances are she'll be able to tell you what's really going on and then the two of you can tackle the problem together. Nevertheless, if during the course of your discussion you sense, not just from her words, but from her overall attitude, that she really doesn't like your son, then trust your "gut" feeling. Take the necessary steps to get your boy's class changed. Teachers are human beings. And some teachers—for whatever reason, rational or irrational—simply don't like certain children. It's nobody's fault. But no child should have to spend his days sitting in a classroom with a teacher who dislikes him.

A Story from a Parent

THIS STORY IS FROM A PARENT OF A GIFTED CHILD WHO FOUND A way to work with a rigid teacher.

When Robin entered fifth grade, she seemed to lose all interest in school. From talking to her I got the impression she was just plain bored. According to Robin (who reads at a ninth-grade level), her teacher, Mrs. Post, insists that she read the same book as the other kids and that she *never,* under any circumstances, read ahead. I reminded her that it was still very early in the term and urged her to be patient. But I really became concerned when she started complaining about headaches and looking for any excuse to avoid going to school.

I called her teacher and made an appointment to see her. The conference did not go well. I told Mrs.

Post that I felt that Robin needed more of a challenge. Mrs. Post told me that what Robin needed was more self-control. According to her, Robin was restless and constantly distracting the other kids who were trying to do their work. I said, "Maybe she's restless because she's finished early and has time on her hands. Maybe she could be given some advanced reading materials."

Mrs. Post looked annoyed and informed me that there was no reason for Robin to be doing different work from the other children. She also let me know that she had been teaching for twenty-three years and that the district-adopted curriculum was very effective in teaching the basics. I almost said, "That's just the point. Robin knows the basics. What harm would there be in giving her some enrichment?" But I didn't. I bit my tongue, thanked her politely, and went home feeling rotten.

When I told my husband about the conference, he said, "Mrs. Post probably thinks you're one of those 'pushy' parents. Maybe you ought to speak to the principal about changing Robin's class."

I considered his suggestion seriously, but the more I thought about it, the more I felt it would be wrong to take Robin away from her friends. The next morning I awoke knowing I had to find some way to help my daughter without offending her teacher. I called my sister-in-law, who is an elementary school teacher, and told her what was going on. She muttered something about teachers who were still in the Dark Ages and then told me about the program she used with the advanced readers in her class. She recommended some book titles for Robin and mentioned a book for teachers that gave some easy ways to evaluate the reading of a student who was doing independent work. It was called *Responding to Literature*.[1] I wrote down everything she said and then went out and bought the book.

The following week I called Mrs. Post and asked if I could see her again. She sounded cool and reserved and said that we had already had our conference. She didn't see the need for another. I told her that it was important to me to speak to her again. Finally she agreed.

When the time came, I was very nervous. I didn't want to do anything to antagonize Mrs. Post again. I started by telling her how disturbed I was to learn about Robin's "acting out" in class and how worried I was about her recent change in attitude toward school. Then I told her I'd been trying to gather some ideas that might possibly help the situation and asked if she'd like to see some of them that I had written out on this paper.

Mrs. Post didn't take the paper I held out to her. She continued to sit with her hand over her mouth. So I picked out a few of the items on my list and read them to her—like having Robin write a different ending to the book everyone was reading, or having her read other books by the same author and share what she had learned with her classmates. I also held up my copy of the book my sister-in-law had recommended—without mentioning where I'd heard about it.

Finally I said, "Mrs. Post, I'm at my wit's end. I just don't know what to do to help Robin. That's why

[1]Sandra M. Simons, *Responding to Literature: Writing and Thinking Activities* (Eugene, Ore.: Spring Street Press, 1990).

I asked for another conference. I wanted to hear what you thought of all these suggestions and I also thought that with all your years of experience, you'd probably have many other ideas." Before Mrs. Post could say a word, I added, "And I'm going to speak to Robin about fooling around in class. No matter how restless she is, you shouldn't have to deal with that."

Mrs. Post continued to look at me in stony silence. Then she stood up and said, "I heard what you had to say and I will take your ideas under consideration." Then she asked if she could borrow the book (I couldn't believe it!) and thanked me for coming. We shook hands. The conference was over. That was a month ago. I have no idea what Mrs. Post is doing in class. All I know is that Robin seems to be enjoying school again. And her morning headaches have disappeared.

Questions from Teachers

1. Some parents seem to have a school phobia. They hate to come to conferences, because bad memories of their own school days come flooding back. Is there any way to help these parents feel more comfortable?

A warm, welcoming attitude is probably the best antidote to their anxieties. Some teachers have found that a table with a cloth, a pot of tea or coffee, and an adult-size chair can help create a friendly mood. Parents report that they especially appreciate a closed door. It signals respect for the private time they spend with you.

2. If parents are divorced, which one should I invite to the conference?

Invite both of them so that neither one feels ignored or shut out. It's up to the parents to decide whether they would prefer to meet with the teacher together or separately. In either case, it's important to use the conference time to focus the discussion not on their relationship but on how, singly or jointly, they can both do what's best for *their* child.

3. What can I do if a parent comes to a conference in a hostile or aggressive mood?

Resist the natural urge to "reason with" the parent's anger: Instead of "Please try to calm down, Mr. Smith. We'll get nowhere if you keep on yelling," acknowledge Mr. Smith's feelings. Let him know you understand the intensity of his emotions: "I can see how angry you are. Please come in and sit down. I want to hear what's on your mind." This kind of approach is more likely to defuse Mr. Smith's strong feelings and to enable him to tell you what's upsetting him.

You may want to consider writing down each of his grievances and reading them back to him so that he knows you understand. If, despite your best efforts, his rage persists, you can reschedule your conference: "Mr. Smith, I can see you're still very upset. I need more time to think about what you've told me. I may even want to consult with other people on the staff. When can we meet again?" At your next meeting you might want to have a third party present—either the principal, the guidance counselor, or the school psychologist.

4. Some parents have complained to me that they hear from teachers only when there's trouble. I

must admit they have a point. Is there any way around this?

Parents appreciate hearing a little "good news." One teacher said he makes it his business at the beginning of the year, while the kids are still on their best behavior and just beginning their academic tasks, to call two parents a night. He highlights each student's strengths and efforts. Then later in the year, if a problem arises, the lines of communication have already been opened and the parents are much more receptive to hearing about any problems that may have arisen.

5. How do I end a conference gracefully with a parent who goes on and on while other parents are waiting outside?

It's important that the parent not feel that a timer has gone off and that he or she is being dismissed. You need to keep an eye on the clock and give some advance notice: "I see we have five minutes left. Is there anything else you want me to know?" If at the end of five minutes there's still more to be explored, you might say, "I wish we had more time. Shall we talk on the phone or schedule another conference?" Have your calendar open and be ready to set another date.

A Story from a Teacher

THIS ACCOUNT WAS REPORTED BY A RESOURCE ROOM TEACHER IN an elementary school.

When Christopher Boyle was assigned to my class in second grade, I could see immediately that he was a bright, articulate boy. But it also became clear when I tested him that he had the classic signs of dyslexia. He couldn't even write his own name without leaving out letters or reversing them. What I didn't understand was why he was such a behavior problem—belligerent, moody, easily upset.

After a few weeks I decided to call his mother to see if she could help me. She was more than willing to meet with me and offered to come in that very afternoon. Almost as soon as we sat down, Mrs. Boyle described how every night Christopher would sit at his desk and try to do his homework and cry and say how dumb he was.

Suddenly I understood what was going on. He was mad because he was convinced he was dumb and was taking it out on himself and everyone else. I explained to Mrs. Boyle that Christopher was far from dumb and that he was, in fact, a very bright boy who expressed curiosity about many things, but because of his dyslexia, he had to overcome problems most children didn't have. I also told her that Christopher was applying himself in my class and that in time I believed that he would learn to read.

Mrs. Boyle seemed cheered by my assessment and asked what she could do to help. I told her that what Christopher needed from her was her understanding of his frustration and her confidence that, slowly but surely, he *would* make progress. I also told her that Christopher had an inquiring mind and would probably benefit from a trip to the library, where he could take out picture books on subjects that interested him.

As the term wore on, it turned out that Christopher was a hard worker. I taught him one phonetic skill at a time and showed him how to sound out words and all the tricks he could use to differentiate one letter from another. And little by little he did learn to read and spell.

All during this time I'd call his mother with progress reports and let her know that what she was doing with Christopher at home was showing in class. She did everything I recommended and more. She encouraged his interest in fish, insects, and rocks. (He was always collecting rocks and asking what they were.) She took him to museums and read books with him and talked with him about all the subjects that fascinated him.

What I did that was especially helpful to Christopher was to bring out into the open the fact that he did have a disability. The hardest thing for him was seeing other kids who were clearly not his intellectual equal read and write and spell with ease and get hundreds on tests that he failed. I wanted him to know that he was a highly intelligent person who was struggling against a learning problem called dyslexia. So I would say to him, "Christopher, it's a big challenge for you to do this spelling, because when other kids look at a *b* they see a *b*, but when you see a *b* your eyes sometimes fool you and it looks like a *d*. So it makes everything more difficult.

It's called dyslexia. But you've worked so hard that you've learned it all anyway."

Christopher really liked talking about his "learning problem." He'd say to the other kids, "See, I have dyslexia. When I look at the word *saw,* I see the word *was.*" And he'd write a word backward on purpose, laugh, hold it up to a mirror to show how the word came out frontward, and boast that he could do "mirror writing." He was taking control of his disability, seeing it as something special and funny that he had.

At our end-of-the-term conference his mother told me that he was like a different child at home. Much happier, much more relaxed. She described how at a family get-together Christopher was playing school with his younger cousin who was also dyslexic. The cousin was becoming agitated because he was trying to write a word and having trouble. Christopher said, "Don't worry. I used to have that problem. I can help you. Let me show you this trick."

Christopher is now in third grade. His teachers tell me he's still reading slowly, but that he always participates, always has something interesting to say, and if they give him a little extra time, he does well on his tests.

Whenever I think about Christopher, I feel good. Between his mother and me, we helped him see that his dyslexia was a challenge that he could overcome, rather than a disability that could define and defeat him.

A Parent and
Teacher Story

THE PREVIOUS STORY DESCRIBED HOW TEAMWORK BETWEEN ONE parent and one teacher affected one child. This final story describes what happened when one school made a concerted effort to reach out to all the parents in a community and involve them in their children's education.

My first teaching assignment was in a rural community of 710 people. Other than a country store and a two-pump gas station, the only community activity that took place was at the school. Given this, I thought parents would flock to PTA meetings and parent conferences. Not so. On our first orientation night the auditorium was practically empty. A grand total of 15 parents showed up. Considering that we had 139 students enrolled in the school, I thought it was a terrible turnout.

The next morning I expressed my disappointment to one of my colleagues and she told me that after a while I'd get used to it. That seemed like a pretty defeatist attitude to me. At the end of our next teachers' meeting, I asked if anyone would be interested in trying to get more parents involved in school activities. A few people chuckled and shook their heads. Somebody said something about me wasting my time and the principal gave me a fatherly smile. When the meeting was over, I felt very foolish. But afterward two teachers, Margaret and Pat, came up to me and volunteered to help. I think they felt sorry for me.

The next day the three of us met after school to see if we could develop a plan. Pat told me what had been tried before and failed: The flyers never made it home. The "telephone tree" (each teacher calling ten families) didn't succeed because many of the parents didn't have phones. Even the barbecue at Margaret's house was a bust. She said she'd invited twenty-four kids and their parents, but only six people came. I had to admit that was all pretty discouraging.

Nevertheless, we decided to go ahead and plan a monthly activity that would somehow get parents more involved in the school. Our first function was a dessert social. (Brownies and cookies supplied by the home economics class and ingredients supplied by the three of us.) We mailed invitations to parents, placed flyers at the store, gas station, and volunteer fire department, and encouraged teachers to attend. The turnout was small, but at the end we recruited the help of two more teachers and eight parents. Even the principal expressed appreciation for our efforts.

The next month we hosted a "Spaghetti Feed" before the Friday night football game and had terrific results. Using the home economics room, five teachers and eight parents cooked enough spaghetti for approximately one hundred people. Granted, most of those who ate were players from both teams and their parents and relatives, but everyone had a good time. Before the evening was over, I grabbed a microphone and announced that on Monday night we were having a meeting to plan our next event and that we needed all the help we could get. Five more parents and three more teachers signed on. The wall that separated teachers and parents began to crack and crumble.

At our Monday meeting one of the parents suggested that we write a monthly newsletter to keep the community informed of school activities. The principal was so impressed with the idea that he offered to fund the postage. The school's secretary volunteered to do the typing and copying. Parents and teachers offered to meet in the school's library to fold, staple, and address the newsletters.

Those newsletters turned the tide. They became the communication link between us and the community. Teachers used them to express their concerns and so did the parents. For example, we found out that some of the parents were very worried about their teenagers driving thirty miles to a larger town on weekends to find entertainment and ending up having accidents because of drinking and driving. A few of the teachers volunteered to chaperone dances or other activities so that the kids would stay in the community.

Once the parents knew that the school wanted their input and help, they came up with ideas that went beyond our wildest expectations. They organized and sponsored a hot lunch program. (Our school had no funds to establish its own.) They hosted a carnival night and transformed the gym into an amusement park with game booths. They volunteered to help out in the classroom and became an invaluable resource. Mothers worked with children in the elementary school classes; a father taught a mini-course in mechanical drafting to the sophomores; another father, who was a chef, gave a demonstration for the home economics class. A group of parents, teachers, and students formed a "Project Graduation" committee and worked at fund-raising all year to earn enough money to send the graduating seniors and chaperones on a chartered bus for a three-day trip to Disneyland. The seniors had a great time and the parents were relieved because their eighteen-year-olds weren't celebrating their graduation by drinking and driving.

The support and involvement of the parents inspired the teachers to do even more. When Margaret discovered that some of the parents couldn't read, she organized a reading class for them. The class was such a hit that the one evening grew into a full adult education program, where parents could also learn writing, cooking, sewing and computer skills. One of the teachers offered a night class for parents who wanted to earn their GED and that, too, was soon filled. Everyone who took the class said their children were so inspired by seeing Mom or Dad study and do homework that their grades improved.

The principal became our most enthusiastic supporter. It was his idea to institute a home visitation program for those parents whom we still hadn't reached. In our newsletter we announced that teachers would be stopping by the homes of their students for brief visits. Each teacher was given the names of approximately eight to ten students and asked to visit their parents at least once in the semester. Pat had the brilliant idea of using our own school buses for transportation. So each Thursday after school, teachers who wanted to visit a family could ride the bus with their students to their homes. At the end of the route, bus drivers would wait thirty minutes before doubling back to pick up teachers. The program was a huge success. Those visits by the teachers seemed to mean a lot to both parents and students.

On the night of the last PTA meeting of the year, I came early because I wanted to run off some handouts for the parents. By the time I was finished, I heard the principal's booming voice and realized that the meeting had begun. I thought I'd slip quietly into an empty seat, but when I opened the door to the auditorium, I gasped. There wasn't an empty seat in the house. The room was packed with parents. They had turned out in full force to be part of the action at *their school.*

The Dream Catcher

IT WAS THE LAST DAY OF SCHOOL. THE LARGE YELLOW BUSES WITH SCHOOL DISTRICT 71 EMBLAZONED on their sides pulled up to the curb. As teachers dismissed their classes, students poured from the open school doors and rushed toward buses that were already bursting with clamoring children. Cars lined the streets with eager parents searching for their offspring and honking recognition.

Mine was the last class to leave. The sun was very bright and the pavement hot. Waves of June heat hit my face. I hated saying good-bye. These children who had filled my days and my thoughts at night had become very dear to me. But with each farewell hug, it struck me anew that my time with them had come to an end. We would never again be connected in the same way.

I stood there waving until the last child was claimed by the last parent. Then I turned and walked back into the nearly deserted building. Once inside my classroom I sat at my desk and looked out at the empty, silent room. No one in the seats; nothing on the bulletin boards; not even a scrap of paper on the floor. It had been a whole year of planning and thinking and worrying and teaching. And now it was over. Finished. Did anything remain—aside from a few memories?

There was a soft knock at the door. It was Roy Schultz.

"Hi, Roy. Did you forget something?"

He shook his head and stood there, a strange expression on his face. What did he want? A final, private goodbye? His mother had called me earlier in the week and poured out all her concerns: She had lost her job at the mill; she and Roy were going to have to move to Chicago and stay with her sister; she didn't know if she could find work there; her sister lived in a bad neighborhood with street gangs; Roy was giving her a hard time about moving; he didn't want to start all over again in a new school.

"Come on in, Roy."

"I missed my bus."

"Oh. Do you need a ride?"

"Nah, I'll walk. . . . Can I tell you something?"

"Sure. Come in. Sit down."

As he edged into a seat across from me, I caught my breath. Under his shirt he was wearing the "dream catcher" I'd given him the day before. The circle of leather with a spiderlike web of string inside it had been my parting gift to Roy. I explained to him that according to Native American legend, if it were hung over the bed of a sleeping person, it would catch all of the bad dreams and the bad spirits and let only the good ones in. I told Roy I wanted him to have it so that he would know that we were thinking of him wherever he was, and he had taken it from me with great solemnity.

At that moment I knew he understood why I was giving it to him, even though until then I hadn't known myself. The dream catcher was my way of sending him off with some measure of protection. Roy had grown so much over the year—and not just in height or heft. He had stopped the name-calling and the racial slurs; he had made a monumental effort to stop cursing; he had stopped bullying and boasting. He bore little resemblance to the tough, angry kid who had swaggered into my room at the beginning of the term wearing a jacket with a skull-and-crossbones patch and looking as if he were spoiling for a fight. Now he was the student most often requested by other teachers as a peer tutor for the "difficult" children because Roy could "manage them."

What would happen to him now? What would happen to all his hard-won progress? How would he react to a hostile environment? Would he revert? Why wouldn't he? Why wouldn't any child?

"What was it you wanted to tell me, Roy?"

"My cousin, he lives in this building I'm moving to, and he says when you live there, you gotta join a gang."

"Got to?"

"Yeah, for protection."

"Against what?"

"Against kids who want to beat you up."

"Oh. So you'd be under a lot of pressure to join."

"Yeah, but maybe I can make other friends."

"You've certainly made a lot of friends in this class."

"Uh-huh."

"I guess you've got a tough decision ahead of you."

"I know. But I'm not gonna join no gang. I don't wanna do that kinda stuff anymore. I just wanted to tell you that." Then he shook my hand and left.

I was overwhelmed. This eleven-year-old boy had been wrestling with a decision that would have shaken a grown man and he had opted to take the higher, harder road. Fervently I wished there were more that I could do for him. Moments later as I gathered my belongings to leave, it occurred to me that maybe, just maybe, I'd done it already.

Maybe the values I had tried to encourage within these

four walls had gone inside Roy and become a part of him. And maybe those values would keep him from harm's way and help him to survive and cope.

Maybe the spirit that I had tried to bring into my classroom was the real "dream catcher" that would protect *all* the children.

Maybe out of the hundreds of hours and thousands of exchanges we had had with each other, something would remain that would safeguard and sustain them—a core experience that would leave them stronger, more compassionate, more able to think and learn and love.

Anyway, I'd like to think so.

ADDITIONAL READING THAT MAY BE HELPFUL

Bluestein, Jane. *Twenty-first-Century Discipline.* Jefferson City, Mo.: Scholastic, 1988.

Branden, Nathaniel. *The Six Pillars of Self-Esteem.* New York: Bantam Books, 1994.

Elkind, David, Ph.D. *Parenting Your Teenager in the Nineties.* Rosemont, N.J.: Modern Learning Press, 1993.

Faber, Adele, and Elaine Mazlish. *How to Talk So Kids Will Listen and Listen So Kids Will Talk.* New York: Rawson, Wade Publishers, Inc., 1980.

———. *Siblings Without Rivalry.* New York: W.W. Norton & Company, 1987.

Gardner, Howard. *Frames of Mind: The Theory of Multiple Intelligence.* New York: Basic Books, 1993.

Ginott, Haim G. *Teacher and Child.* New York: Avon Books, 1970.

Gordon, Thomas. *Teaching Children Self-Discipline at Home and in School.* New York: Random House, 1989.

———. *Teacher Effectiveness Training.* New York: Peter H. Wyden, 1974.

Healy, Jane M. *Is Your Bed Still There When You Close the Door? And Other Playful Ponderings.* New York: Doubleday, 1992.

Hyman, Irwin A. *Reading, Writing, and the Hickory Stick.* Lexington, Mass.: Lexington Books, 1990.

Kohn, Alfie. *Punished by Rewards.* Boston: Houghton Mifflin Company, 1993.

Kurcinka, Mary Sheedy. *Raising Your Spirited Child.* New York: HarperCollins, 1991.

Levin, Diane. *Teaching Young Children in Violent Times: Building a Peaceable Classroom.* Cambridge, Mass.: Educators for Social Responsibility, 1994.

Webster-Doyle, Terrence. *Why Is Everybody Always Picking on Me?* Middlebury, Vt.: Atrium Society Publications, 1991.

Wlodkowski, Raymond J., and Judith H. Jaynes. *Eager to Learn: Helping Children Become Motivated and Love Learning.* San Francisco: Jossey-Bass, 1991.

INDEX

orders, 61–62, 63, 90

parent-teacher conferences,
229–62
children present at, 245–46
with divorced parents, 253
for educationally advanced
children, 249–52
for educationally delayed children, 248, 255–57
ending of, 254
hostile parents in, 253
increasing parental participation
in, 258–62
negative assessment of children in, 247
positive focus in, 253–54
questions from parents about,
245–49
questions from teachers
about, 252–54
stories from parents about,
249–52, 258–62
stories from teachers about,
255–62
on strained student-teacher
relationships, 248–49
peer pressure, 154–55
permissiveness, 53
personality, innate, 224
philosophical response to feelings, 26
pity, 26, 46–47
"please formula," 85
positive feedback, *see* praise, descriptive
posttraumatic stress symptoms,
122–23
praise, descriptive, 165–93
evaluation vs., 169–70, 176,
183–85
excessive amounts of, 180
potential effects of, 181–82
questions from parents about,
180–83
questions from teachers
about, 188–90
stories from parents about,
183–88

stories from teachers about,
191–93
unacceptable behavior and,
191–92
problem solving, 129–64
brainstorming in, 150–51,
157–58
with humor, 76, 79–81,
87–88
offering choices in, 86, 92–93,
126–27
points of view and, 124–25,
150
questions from parents about,
150–52
questions from teachers
about, 156–59
six steps for, 130–31, 136, 149,
156
stories from parents about,
152–55
stories from teachers about,
159–64
writing in, 85–86, 88, 89,
94–96, 124–25, 157
prophesying, 65
PTA (Parent-Teacher Association), 258, 262
punishment, 97–128
alternatives to, 113
corporal, 99, 101, 117–18,
127–28
as deterrent to misconduct,
101
group, 117
long-term effects of,
122–23
questions from parents about,
114–18
questions from teachers
about, 122–25
rewards vs., 114
stories from parents about,
119–22
stories from teachers about,
125–28
time-out, 115–16

questioning, of children, 26, 52

271

rage, acknowledgment of, 55–56, 124–25
rap music, 93–94
Reading, Writing, and the Hickory Stick (Hyman), 122
respect:
  for children, 84, 123–24, 136
  for teachers and parents, 233–34
rewards, punishment vs., 114
roles, 194–228
  avoidance of, 216–17
  freeing students from, 201–9, 215
  locking students in, 217
  positive aspects of, 216
  questions from parents about, 216–17
  questions from teachers about, 222–24
  stories from parents about, 218–21
  story from a teacher about, 224–28
  teacher expectations and, 222, 223–24

Sabatino, Ann C., 100*n*
Sabatino, David A., 100*n*
sarcasm, in teachers, 64–65
school anxiety, 45, 48–50
school plays, 102–3, 108
scolding, 91–92, 185–86
self-esteem, 189
self-image, 196–99
  see also roles
separation anxiety, 153–54
shyness, 246–47
siblings:
  praising individual achievements of, 182–83
  roles of, 219–20
silence in children, 47

Simons, Sandra M., 251
sleep troubles, 123
star students, 189
stuttering, 123

talking in class, 90–91, 197–98
task orientation, 181
teachers:
  in counseling roles, 52
  expectations of, 222, 223–24
  as martyrs, 64
  testing of, 53
  see also parent-teacher conferences
teacher's pets, 188–89
teasing, 94–96, 151–52
teenagers, 89–90
television watching, 142, 148
temper, adult loss of, 116–17
Templeton, Rosalyn, 15–16
threats, 63
throwaways, 220–21
time-out, 115–16
tone of voice, 84
"troublemakers," 222

values, encouragement of, 263–66
violence, in schools, 14–15, 16–17, 158–59, 223–24

war, as source of collective anxiety, 56–58
warnings, from teacher, 64
writing, 89
  as alternative to punishment, 124–25
  and being teased, 94–96
  for forgetfulness, 85–86, 88, 156–57
  and school anxiety, 48–49

"you," in accusations, 150